Pope [illegible] THEOLOGICAL JOURNEY

to the

PRAYER MEETING OF RELIGIONS IN ASSISI

Part II, Volume 2

The "Trinitarian Trilogy"

Redemptor Hominis, Dives in Misericordia, Dominum et Vivificantem

Fr. Johannes Dörmann

ANGELUS PRESS
2918 Tracy Avenue, Kansas City, Missouri 64109

Pope John Paul II's Theological Journey to the Prayer Meeting of Religions in Assisi

Part II, Volume 2

Second Encyclical: *Dives in Misericordia*

Fr. Johannes Dörmann

Translated from the German for Angelus Press, with permission from the author, by Rev. Sebastian Wall, with reference research by Peter Chojnowski, Ph.D. At the translator's wish, the classical English forms have been retained.

ANGELUS PRESS
2918 TRACY AVENUE
KANSAS CITY, MISSOURI 64109
PHONE (816) 753-3150
FAX (816) 753-3557
ORDER LINE (800) 966-7337

ISBN 0-935952-72-1 Part II, Volume 2
ISBN 0-935952-57-8 Set
FIRST PRINTING—November 1998

Printed in the United States of America

Library of Congress Cataloging-in-Publication Data

Dörmann, Johannes, 1922-
[Theologische Weg Johannes Pauls II zum Weltgebetstag der Religionen in Assisi. English]
Pope John Paul II's Theological Journey to the Prayer Meeting of Religions at Assisi / Johannes Dörmann.
p. cm.
Translation of: *Der theologische Weg Johannes Pauls II zum Weltgebetstag der Religionen in Assisi.*
Contents: pt. 2. Volume 2.
Includes bibliographical references.
ISBN 0-935952-52-7 (v. 1 : pbk.)
1. John Paul II, Pope, 1920- . 2. Catholic Church–Doctrines–History–20th century. 3. Swiatowy Dzień Modlitwy o Pokój (1986 : Assisi, Italy) 4. Swiatowy Dzień Modlitwy o Pokój (1986 : Assisi, Italy) I. Title.
BX1378.4.D6713 1994 261.2–dc20 94-25185 CIP
10 9 8 7 6 5 4 3 2

CONTENTS

FOREWORD

The second part does not contain two volumes, as was originally planned, but three. The first volume deals with the Encyclical *Redemptor Hominis* [= *RH*], this second volume, *Dives in Misericordia* [= *DiM*], and the third *Dominum et Vivificantem* [= *DeV*].

The subject is still very much up to date. "Assisi 1986" was followed up by the subsequent meetings at Kyoto (1987), Rome (1988), Warsaw (1989), Bari (1990), Malta (1991) and finally in Brussels on the 14th-15th September 1992. The second prayer meeting with the Pope in Assisi (9th-10th January 1993) to which John Paul II and the presidents of the European bishops' conferences on the 1st December also invited "the other churches and Christian communities in Europe" as well as the Jews and Moslems, was meant "in a certain way to renew the remarkable meeting of the 27th October 1986" and "to be, as it were, a symbol and focus of prayer for all men of good will."[1] It was a sign of the new way in which Europe was to be evangelised. The original enthusiasm for united and inter-religious prayer for peace of the first meeting was, however, lacking. The planned prayer meeting in Jerusalem for September 1994 ought to have a new symbolic quality.[2]

It is quite possible to say with Francis Cardinal Arinze, the president of the Pontifical Council for Inter-Religious Dia-

---

1 Cf. *L'Osservatore Romano*, English edition [hereafter abbreviated to *OR*, Eng.] from 9th December 1992, documents p. 1 (*Assisi — On the Way to Peace, Call of John Paul II and the Presidents of the European Bishops' Conferences for a Day of Prayer for Peace in Europe*).

2 See *OR*, Eng., from 13th January 1993, p. 1 and 2ff. — Guido Horst, *Deutsche Tagespost*, 12th January 1993, p.3. — Lucio Brunelli, *30 Days*, January 1993, p. 11ff. — Concerning the meeting in Jerusalem see

logue, that John Paul II has made inter-religious dialogue "a mark of his pontificate." Such a dialogue is, as the Cardinal said in his speech in Nuremberg on 14th April 1989,

> a meeting of heart and spirit between the followers of the different religions. It is a spiritual exchange between two believers on a religious plane. It is a joint journey to the truth and a working together on projects of common interest. It is an absolute religious partnership with no hidden aims or motives.

The high point of inter-religious dialogue is of course praying together, which John Paul II already put forward as the aim of his pontificate in his inaugural Encyclical (cf. *RH* 6,3) and put into practise for the first time in the history of the Church on 27th October 1986.[3]

In his message on 19th September 1992 to the sixth follow-up meeting in Brussels the Pope mentioned to the president of the Pontifical Council for Christian Unity, Edward Idris Cardinal Cassidy, how happy, grateful and joyful he is about inter-religious prayer for peace. He feels himself obliged to continue in the spirit of the first meeting at Assisi and asks everyone to live and spread the "spirit of Assisi."[4] In this message John Paul II explains again how he sees the essence of this

---

Paulinus, 13th February 1994: "The next international prayer meeting of the world's religions for peace will be in September 1994 in Jerusalem. The yearly meeting which not only representatives of the various Christian churches but also Jews, Moslems, Buddhists and Animists take part in, is part of the tradition of the first inter-religious prayer for peace to which Pope John Paul II invited everyone to Assisi in 1986."

[3] Johannes Dörmann, *Die eine Wahrheit und die vielen Religionen*. [*The One Truth and the Many Religions*]. — *Assisi: Anfang einer neuen Zeit* [*Assisi: Beginning of a new Age*] (Abensberg, 1988), pp. 125-182. Furthermore: *Theological Journey* [*Der theologische Weg*] Part I, pp. 15ff.; 26ff. and Part II/1, pp. 5ff.

[4] *OR*, Eng., 23rd September 1992, pp. 1-2.

prayer meeting of the religions and how he wants it to be understood. The authentic interpretation of the Pope is as follows:

> The prayer meetings themselves show more clearly the solidarity of the faithful of the various religions between themselves and are a sign for the world. They are an example and an encouragement for more understanding between peoples. The religions must be aware of their responsibility of working for the unity of humanity.
>
> Prayer is the bond that unites most effectively because, thanks to it, the faithful meet each other where inequality, misunderstanding, resentment and enmities are overcome, namely before God, the Lord and Father of all. In so far as it is a true expression of the correct relationship with God and one's fellow man, it is already a positive contribution towards peace (Message to the 25th World day of peace, no. 4).[5]

According to the text "inequalities" are overcome in prayer before God, the Lord and Father of all. The Pope had already given the reason why he thinks this in his talk to the cardinals on 22nd December 1986 and he repeated it in his Encyclical *Redemptoris Missio* (Art. 29), "The meeting of religions in Assisi intended to emphasise clearly my conviction that 'all authentic prayer is from the Holy Ghost Who in a mysterious way is present in the heart of every man.'"[6] "Authentic prayer" meant concretely, in Assisi 1986, the representatives of the religions, in "radical faithfulness" to their respective "traditions" offering their "prayers" to their "divinities." Nonetheless these "prayers" were inspired by the Holy Ghost because He is "present in the heart of every man." In the end it is this con-

---

5 *Ibid.*

6 *Redemptoris Missio* (7th December 1990), *Deutsche Tagespost*, 24th January 1991, p. 8 — Pope's talk to cardinals of 22nd December 1986, 11 AAS 79 (1987), 1089.

viction of the Pope which is the reason behind the inter-religious prayers for peace. According to the Gospel, however, the Father and the Son sent the Holy Ghost as fruit of the Redemption into the hearts of Christ's disciples (Jn. 15:26f; 16:5ff.), in Whom we may say "Abba," Father. (cf. Rom. 8:15ff).

At his general audience at Castel Gandolfo on 9th September 1992 the Pope justified his generous interpretation of what authentic prayer is with reference to the well-known "restless heart" of St. Augustine and continued, "That is why the experience of prayer is a basic act common to believers of all religions, even those where the belief in God as a person has either completely disappeared or is obscured by false representations."[7]

From this point of view, inter-religious prayer which overcomes all differences is already a sign of the unity in the Holy Ghost of the believers of all religions.[8] It was this conviction which made the Pope invite representatives of the world's religions to pray for peace in Assisi. This invitation alone is recognition enough of the power of the prayer of all religions to their various *Numina* to bring about peace; it also recognises the non-Christian religions as paths of salvation and means of revealing God.

The declared intention of the inter-religious prayer meeting in the "spirit of Assisi" is the "unity of mankind" which is supposed to be an implicit reality in the authentic prayer of all religions and therefore a "positive contribution towards peace."

This is an extraordinary viewpoint for the Pope to have. It does not take much to see how unrealistic an "*interpretatio christiana*" of completely different religious realities is. At the root of the Pope's behaviour lies his inadmissible generalisation of the following hypotheses which are simply in complete con-

---

[7] *OR*, Eng. of 16th September 1992.

[8] Already in *Sign of Contradiction* [*Zeichen des Widerspruchs*] (Seabury Press, New York, 1979), p. 19ff. — cf. Part I, pp. 49-59.

tradiction with historical reality:

– The most effective bond of solidarity between the believers of all religions is prayer. But such a bond is nonexistent since each religion understands something else by the word "prayer." The way of Buddha to enlightenment is self-Redemption, submersion (*jhana*), not "prayer."

– The followers of very different religions are called "faithful" or "believers." But depending on their religion they have a very different concept of what "Faith" is. It is impossible to generalise the uniqueness of faith in Christ which is the foundation of the specifically Christian belief.

– The "believers" of all religions meet in prayer before "God, the Lord and Father of all" and by this overcome their differences. But precisely in their "prayers" it is not before the one God of biblical revelation, the only "Lord and Father of all" that they stand but they turn to their own particular, very different "divinities." Many not only have a "rather indistinct view of God as a person" but refuse even to recognise a personal God and Creator as Lord and Father.

– All religions have the "historical responsibility" of working for the "unity of mankind." But this *per se* political, Freemasonic aim is not only foreign to the essence of Christianity but also to other religions.

The radical differences between the historical religions are not an obstacle for the Pope to talk about a "common experience of prayer" of the "believers of all religions" and about an "authentic prayer" of everyone in the Holy Ghost to God, "the Lord and Father of all."

The Pope's extremely subjective view quite simply ignores the given reality of historical religions. It places radically different realities under one Christian umbrella and thus puts forward an identity which simply does not exist.

The "God of Assisi" is not the God of the Bible. In the inter-religious prayer to the "one" God of all religions in the "unity of the believers of all religions" it is not just a question of making a hypothesis of the Pope a reality which is at odds with it. It is a matter of the First Commandment!

Seen dogmatically the Pope's teachings and praxis are a complete *novum* for the Catholic Church. They are contradictory to the whole of Sacred Scripture and Tradition. It is unthinkable that a Pope before the Second Vatican Council would have closed his English address to the Head of State in the capital of an Islamic country in which Christians are bloodily persecuted and repressed under Islamic law in the name of Allah with the blessing "Baraka Allah as-Sudan" (Allah = God bless the Sudan) calling down Allah's blessing on that country.[9] For the Moslem Allah is the God of the Koran. A Moslem would have to understand the Pope's intercessory prayer in Arabic as a confirmation of the legitimate spreading of Islam in the name of Allah.

By calling upon people to live and spread the "spirit of Assisi" the Pope has breathed this spirit into his own conciliar Church and her mission. The "spirit of Assisi" has long since seeped into the inner sanctuary of the Church, the celebration of the Eucharist. A clear expression of this may be found in the "prayer from India" which was printed in *Missio*'s "Suggestions and Elements to Shape the Community Mass" and made a prayer after Communion in Aachen on World Mission Sunday 1992 (p. 11):

---

[9] *OR*, Eng., 17th February 1993, p. 13. It would certainly have been possible to continue in English and in the Christian sense call upon the name of God concerning the terrible happenings in Sudan. — In his talk to the leaders of the various religious communities in Khartoum on 10th February 1993 the Pope said, "Here in Sudan I cannot omit to stress the high regard which the Catholic Church has for the followers of Islam" (*OR*, Eng., 13th February 1993, p. 13). — Since May 1983 there are said to have been over 1.3 million Sudanese killed (cf. *Die katholischen Missionen* [*The Catholic missions*], Aachen, May/June 1994, p. 77).

Lord, you created
the continents.
You made men
differ in language and culture.
You make the rice grow
As long as man can remember.
You are the one
who appears in
the many faces of religions...

The "spirit of Assisi 1986" up to Assisi 1993 is also the spirit of John Paul II's "Trinitarian Theology" on his way to the world day of prayer of the religions in the city of St. Francis.

INTRODUCTION

1. Presentation and method

The same presentation and method as in Part II, Volume 1 which dealt with the inaugural Encyclical will also be used for this commentary.[1]

Dives in Misericordia is a well composed unity. The delicate language, style and composition that appear when the Encyclical is closely examined show how carefully it has been put together. Often the precise meaning of a theological statement is seen only after the whole style and language has been clearly taken into account. It would, however, be outside the scope of this study to give a full stylistic analysis. This will be done by way of example in two particular passages. (see *DiM* 1.1; 3).

The main point of this study is once again to understand the Pope. Karl Lehmann sees no difficulty here. In his Herder commentary on *Dives in Misericordia* he writes,

> Pope John Paul II speaks an especially simple and rousing language in his new Encyclical on divine mercy. That is why it is not necessary to write a detailed commentary explaining each sentence. The text of the Encyclical is mostly self explanatory. A commentary therefore just needs to show the basic perspectives of the links with the Second Vatican Council and earlier statements of the present Pope as well as the importance of this document.[2]

---

[1] Cf. Part II/1, pp. 43-45.

[2] *Der bedrohte Mensch und die Kraft des Erbarmens. Die Enzyklika über das Erbarmen Gottes Papst Johannes Pauls II.* [*Threatened Man and the Power of Mercy. Pope John Paul II's Encyclical on Divine Mercy.*]. Revised German translation and commentary by Karl Lehmann (Freiburg-Basel-Wien 1981).

Lehmann could be underestimating the difficulties of interpretation. Really understanding the Pope means understanding him from his own theological suppositions. These are, however, by no means obvious. John Paul II's *nouvelle théologie* [new theology] has its own theological principles of knowledge and thence its own individual form. That is also why our commentary starts from the Pope's principles of knowledge as they were deduced from *Sign of Contradiction* in Part I.[3] The results will be used as a sure working hypothesis which will nonetheless be adapted to *Dives in Misericordia.*

By looking at the actual words used in the Encyclical we will try to find the main theological points and to show how John Paul II's theology continues to develop in *Dives in Misericordia.* In this way our commentary will accompany the Encyclical.

The extensive quotation of the text of the Encyclical in the theologically fundamental first section of the Encyclical (Ch. I-V) is necessary so that the reader can see in an authentic manner each theological statement, its language and argumentation, together with the Pope's way of looking at things. The way the Pope, because of the theological foundation of his personal concept of revelation, subtly changes the meaning of Sacred Scripture and Tradition can only be seen in longer texts in their context.

2. Plan and layout

The plan and layout of the commentary follow that of *Dives in Misericordia*:

The Encyclical is divided into 8 chapters with 15 articles:

I-V: fundamental theological development of the theme (1-9).

VI: A picture of our generation which is so much in need of divine mercy (10-12).

---

[3] See Part I pp. 47-98. But also Part II/1, pp. 3-36 [entire INTRODUCTION].

VII-VIII: God's mercy in the mission of the Church (13-15).[4]

The edition of the text of the Encyclical follows the official English translation published by the Catholic International News Service.* Often the translation does not accurately convey the sense of the Latin text.[5] Where the English text departs from the Latin original this will be demonstrated by quoting from the original Latin.

---

4 The Latin text has no special title for each chapter or article. The titles of the chapters and articles in the official English translation are only followed in part. Where they differ they are noted. The titles of the individual paragraphs in the main theological section (1-5) have been added.

* Also available from Pauline Books & Media, Boston, MA, *The Mercy of God—Dives in Misericordia* (no date).

5 Cf. the commentary by Karl Lehmann, *op. cit.*, p. 116-118. — Comments on the official English translation will only be made where the Latin original seems to require it.

Dives in Misericordia: Encyclical of Pope John Paul II to the Catholic Church on the Divine Mercy*

Title—Address—Salutation

The title *Dives in Misericordia* contains *in nuce* the whole theological and pastoral programme of the Encyclical. Concerning how mercy is to be understood in the Encyclical Karl Lehmann remarks in his commentary,

> Mercy thus understood can take the world off its hinges. Merciful love is the strongest revolutionary power in the world. In this sense the theme of the Pope's second Encyclical contains an explosive spiritual potential to change inter human relations and also socio-political structures.[1]

The idea of thoroughly changing the world through merciful love is in harmony with the essence of the Christian faith and the mission of the Church.[2] When the love of the

---

* *Litterae Encyclicae Ad Episcopos, Sacerdotes et Christifideles totius Catholicae Ecclesiae: de Divina Misericordia. Joannes Paulus PP. II. — Venerabiles Fratres, Dilecti Filii et Filiae, salutem et Apostolicam Benedictionem.* — AAS Vol. 72 (1980), 1177-1232.

[1] Karl Lehmann, *Der bedrohte Mensch und die Kraft des Erbarmens. Die Enzyklika über das Erbarmen Gottes Papst Johannes Pauls II.* [*Threatened Man and the Power of Mercy. Pope John Paul II's Encyclical on Divine Mercy.*] Revised German translation and commentary by Karl Lehmann (Freiburg-Basel-Wien 1981).

[2] Johannes Dörmann, *Mission und Heilsangebot* [*Mission and the Offer of Salvation*], in Adolf Exeler, (pub.), *Fragen der Kirche heute* [*Questions*

Gospel came into the world it brought with it in fact the "strongest revolutionary power."[3] But it is not simply a matter of the strongest revolutionary power in "the world." The love of the Gospel is of divine origin. It is "not of this world." Bearing in mind "political theology," "liberation theology" and "theology of the revolution" we must be careful. Making brothers of the Gospel of love and the teaching of Marxism and Neomarxism is rather macabre.[4]

In his presentation of the Encyclical Lehmann sees no sign of a misinterpretation of this "revolutionary power" of the Gospel, but rather the joining of the classical social teaching of the Church with the heart of the "Christian good news of Salvation" and in it an enriching of what has been taught so far "in a new dimension."[5] This joining has also been a part of the classical social teaching of the Church but it takes place in the Encyclical through a new definition of mercy and in a completely new way.

Dives in Misericordia is not written, as *Redemptor Hominis* was, for the Church and humanity but only for the "bishops, priests and faithful of the whole Catholic Church." The address is as follows, "Venerable brethren, beloved sons and daughters." An issue is not made of the relationship with the non-Christian religions. Since however the Pope's *nouvelle théologie* is based fundamentally on universal-religious principles *Dives in Misericordia* is another milestone on the way to Assisi.

---

for the Church Today] (Würzburg 1971), pp. 229-236.

[3] Johannes Dörmann, *Die universale Mission der Kirche vor der Herausforderung der einheimischen Kulturen* [*The Church's Universal Mission Faced With the Challenge of Native Cultures*], in Johannes Dörmann, (pub.) *Weltmission in der Weltkrise* [*World Mission in a World Crisis*] (St. Augustin 1978), pp. 9-20.

[4] Johannes Dörmann, *Theologie der Mission?* [*Theology of the Mission*], in *theologie und glaube* [*Theology and Faith*] (Paderborn 1973), pp. 342-361; Johannes Dörmann, series of articles *Kirchliche Basisgemeinden* [*Basic Communities in the Church*], in *Der Fels* [*The Rock*] (Regensburg 1984), No. 2-no. 6.

[5] Karl Lehmann, *op. cit.* p. 112.

CHAPTER I

"Who Sees Me, Sees the Father" (cf. Jn. 14:9)

The first chapter contains in two articles the plan (*DiM* 1) and a sketch (*DiM* 2) of the Encyclical.

1. Plan of the Encyclical *

The Pope first formulates the theme of the Encyclical (*DiM* 1.1), then he shows the relationship with his first Encyclical (*DiM* 1.2-4)

1.1 Theme and main points

The Encyclical begins with the programmatic sentences (*DiM* 1.1):

> "God..., who is full of mercy" (Eph. 2:4), was revealed as a Father by Jesus Christ: it is His very Son who, in Himself, has manifested Him and made Him known to us. (cf. Jn. 1:18; Heb. 1,1ff.). Memorable in this regard is the moment when Philip, one of the twelve Apostles, turned to Christ and said, "Lord, show us the Father, and we shall be satisfied"; and Jesus replied, "Have I been with you so long, and yet you do not know me...? He who has seen me has seen the Father" (cf. Jn. 14:8ff.). These words were spoken during the final discourse at the end of the Paschal meal which was followed by the events of those holy days when it became obvious to everyone that "God..., who is full of mercy, for his

* Title in the English translation, "The Revelation of Mercy." The English translation has no titles for the different sub-articles like this commentary.

> exceeding charity wherewith he loved us, even when we were dead in sins, hath quickened us together in Christ" (Eph. 2:4ff.).

The first sentence gives the theme the second shows the main points.

The English translation of the first sentence is imprecise and does not completely express the fullness of the Latin original. The subtle way in which the Pope constructs his sentences, however, requires a more exact rendering of what is said especially when dealing with this key text of the Encyclical's theme.

The Latin text is as follows: "*Dives in Misericordia Deus* (cf. Eph 2:4) *ipse quidem est nobis quem Christus Iesus revelavit ut Patrem: immo quem ostendit nobis ac demonstravit in sese Filius nempe eius* (cf. Jn. 1:18; Heb. 1:1ff.)." Which literally translated means,

> It is God Himself who is rich in mercy, whom Jesus Christ has revealed as Father, indeed whom the Son showed and made known to us in Himself.

This formulation of the theme gives the point of departure (*Qua in re*) for marking the Encyclical's main point: "Who has seen me has seen the Father."

Theme and emphasis are presented in biblical raiment (Eph. 2:4; Jn. 1:18; 14:8ff.; Heb. 1:1ff.). Nonetheless the formulation of the theme seems on closer inspection rather odd. Why is "*Deus*" moved in the quotation from Scripture Eph. 2:4 (= *Deus autem, qui dives est in misericordia*, becomes *Dives in misericordia Deus*) in connection with the Father who is not mentioned in Eph. 2:4? The following paragraph answers this (*DiM* 1.2).

1.2 "Double revelation": The Encyclical's theological principles of knowledge

The Pope shows the connection and relation of his first Encyclical to *Dives in Misericordia* (*DiM* 1.2):

> Following the teachings of the Second Vatican Council and with reference to the special needs of our time, I dedicated the Encyclical *Redemptor Hominis* to the truth about man who is revealed to us in his fullness and depth in Christ. A need no less important in these critical and by no means easy times requires me to once again go into the mystery of Christ in order to discover in Him the face of the Father who is the "Father of mercy and the God of all consolation" (II Cor 1:3). In the Constitution *Gaudium et Spes* [= *GS*] we read, "Christ the new Adam, fully reveals man to himself and brings to light his most high calling," and he does this "in the very revelation of the mystery of the Father and of his love" (*GS* 22).
>
> The words that I have quoted are clear testimony to the fact that man cannot be manifested in the full dignity of his nature without reference—not only on the level of concepts but also in an integrally existential way—to God. Man and man's lofty calling are revealed in Christ through the revelation of the mystery of the Father and His love.

Dives in Misericordia is based on *Redemptor Hominis.* Both Encyclicals have the same plan.

Fr. R. Tucci the head of Radio Vatican showed in a very striking way the relationship of the two Encyclicals to one another when he presented *Dives in Misericordia* by comparing them with a painting in two parts: the first picture shows man in his great dignity, the second God in His mercy.[1]

This diptych is an organic whole. *Dives in Misericordia* is not only the thematic continuation of *Redemptor Hominis* but also the completion of its organic unity. The mutual ordering of both Encyclicals to each other matches the theological principle of knowledge: the "double revelation."

This principle which Cardinal Wojtyla drew from *Gaudium*

---

[1] *L'Osservatore Romano,* German ed. [hereafter abbreviated to *OR,* dt.] 120 (1980) of 3rd December 1980 (no. 280, pp. 5 & 8).

et Spes (22, 1-2) has been dealt with in detail in vols. I and II/1.[2] That is why it is enough here with reference to the present quoted text to pick out the essential:

The "truth about man" or "the full dignity of his nature" is the "being in Christ" which has been given in an inalienable manner to the whole of humanity without any condition *actu uno* by the act of Creation and each individual man from the first moment of his existence participates in this because the Son of God by His Incarnation has formally united Himself with each man.[3] This "*a priori* revelation" in the depths of human existence is the axiom of universal salvation. The Pope's Encyclical *Redemptor Hominis* is dedicated to this "truth about man." The thesis of universal salvation then is obviously the presupposition of the Encyclical *Dives in Misericordia*.

The "truth about man" is made known in and through Christ by means of the "revelation of the Father and His (merciful) love." The Encyclical *Dives in Misericordia* is dedicated to this historical "*a posteriori* revelation." It makes known to the redeemed man the "full dignity of his nature."

Hence the "double revelation," as Cardinal Wojtyla already stressed, has *per se* an "anthropocentric character."[4]

It is now possible to answer the question which after the proper formulation of the Encyclical's theme was still open. The formulation runs (*DiM* 1.1):

> It is God Himself who is rich in mercy, whom Jesus Christ has revealed as Father, indeed whom the Son showed and made known to us in Himself.

It is clear: the theme agrees with the definition of the "*a posteriori* revelation" and has the same content. Thus the Pope

---

[2] Cf. Part I, pp. 78-123; Part II/1, pp. 18-36.

[3] *Ibid.*

[4] Cf. *Sign of Contradiction,* (Seabury Press, New York, 1979), pp. 117ff.

has already made clear in the first sentence of his Encyclical that *Dives in Misericordia* rests on the foundation of his theological principle of knowledge of the "double revelation" just like *Redemptor Hominis* and must be understood in this way.

The declared aim of the Encyclical, "to discover the face of the Father in the mystery of Christ" is thus the development of the "*a posteriori* revelation" in the sense of the proposed understanding of revelation. What is specific about *Dives in Misericordia* is the stress laid on of the visibility of the Father in Jesus Christ. The quotation, "Who has seen me has seen the Father" (Jn. 14:9), appears many times in important places in the Encyclical (*DiM* 1.1; 4.12; 7.6; 8.6; 13.2). By this central idea the Father is likewise brought into the realm of experience and as it were made the subject of the revelation in the history of salvation.

The "double revelation" principle determines therefore the whole construction of the Encyclical. That is to say, the *a priori* revelation is always presupposed and, therefore, universal salvation. The theme of *Dives in Misericordia* is to be understood in the sense of the historical "*a posteriori* revelation" as a means of interpreting the *a priori* revelation. This suggests a more precise consideration of the well thought out formulation of the theme. It contains three points:

– Jesus Christ has revealed the God rich in mercy as Father.

– The Son has showed Him and made Him known to us in Himself. Hence the emphasis:

– With the words, "Who has seen me has seen the Father" Jesus Christ Himself tells us that we see the God rich in mercy as Father in Him.

The three statements taken in themselves seem to represent the sense of the quotation from St. John's Gospel. But they are to be understood in the sense of the Pope's idea of revelation and have undergone therefore an inner, almost imperceptible change: they are to be taken as a means of communicating the theory of universal salvation.

For a better understanding of the problem and of the matter itself we should ask three questions about the three statements:

– Certainly Christ has made the God rich in mercy known to us as Father. But does that mean that Christ revealed Him simply "as Father" thus "only" as Father?

Christ Himself speaks about God the Father, from "my and from your Father." The Christian terminology presupposes a Trinitarian God and talks therefore about God the Father but also about God the Son and God the Holy Ghost. Christian revelation knows the merciful God not only "as Father" but also "as Son" and "as Holy Ghost." It is dogma that "all God's external activities are common to all three Persons."[5] By the way the theme is formulated the revelation of the merciful God can be reduced to simply "God as Father" and only "as Father." To reduce Christian revelation from a trinitarian God to a "Father God" in such a way would be modalistic.

– The second statement leads in the same direction. Has Christ really made immediately visible for us the God rich in mercy and only "as Father"?

The thought that God has appeared to us in Jesus Christ occurs throughout St. John's Gospel. But it is rather the Son of God made man in whom we see the "glory of God." That is how John the Evangelist gives witness to the divinity of Jesus Christ. The Evangelist already gives the foundation of this divinity in the prologue to his Gospel: The Word, which is God, "became flesh and dwelt amongst us. And we saw His glory, the glory of the only begotten Son of the Father, full of grace and truth" (Jn. 1:14). In faith therefore we see the divine glory of the "only begotten of the Father," not the Father Himself. St. John says the same at the beginning of his first epistle, "That which was from the beginning, which we have heard, which we have seen with our eyes, which we have looked upon,

[5] Ludwig Ott, *Fundamentals of Catholic Dogma* [*Grundiß der katholischen Dogmatik*], trans. Patrick Lynch (Herder Book, St. Louis, 1954), p. 80-81.

and our hands have handled, of the word of life, that we have seen and do bear witness and declare unto you" (I Jn. 1:1). This applies only to the Son not to the Father.

The *Logos*, the eternal Son became flesh and dwelt amongst us, not the Father. The incarnate Son of God offered the redemptive sacrifice on the Cross, not the Father. The redemptive sacrifice is not only the revelation of the Father's love but also the work of the Son which He offered due to His own divine authority and love.

– Did Christ by saying, "Who has seen me has seen the Father" (Jn. 14:9) really only reveal the mystery of "God as Father" and His love?

These majestic words of Jesus are really saying to Philip first of all that the person who is speaking to him is God Himself as His Father is and for that reason embodies for the disciples the essence of the Father as Son. It means that from the knowledge of Jesus Christ knowledge of the Father must necessarily follow. It communicates the essential unity of the Father and the Son (cf. Jn. 10:30). It is not a modalistic statement. The Son is also not only the revealer or the medium of "revelation of the mystery of the Father and His love." The Son Himself is God and reveals Himself through His word and ministry as the consubstantial Son of the Father. Christ Himself tells the apostle Philip how the relationship between the Father and the Son is to be understood, "Do you not believe, that I am in the Father, and the Father in me?" (Jn. 14:10).

The question remains: how are we to understand the redemptive work of Christ if this has already been determined by the Pope's special way of looking at revelation and the theme and emphasis of the Encyclical and if the "truth about man" is "announced" to man in and through Christ only via the revelation of God as Father and His merciful love? The answer is to be found in the Encyclical *Dives in Misericordia.*

Digression: Concerning the artistic way in which the Encyclical is written

Dives in Misericordia is a cleverly composed and well rounded unity. This aspect should be taken into consideration when judging the intention of a particular statement within the text. This is the case for the whole Encyclical but can only be gone into detail in this commentary with two examples. The first example is in the first paragraph of the Encyclical which is reproduced here with some non-essential omissions.

> "It is God Himself who is rich in mercy," (Eph. 2:4) whom Jesus Christ has revealed as Father, indeed whom the Son showed and made known to us in Himself (cf. Jn. 1:18; Heb. 1:1ff.). Memorable in this regard is the moment (*Qua in re*) when Philip,...turns to Jesus with the request, "Lord, show us the Father and it is enough for us," and he receives the answer, "Who has seen me has seen the Father" (cf. Jn. 14:8ff.). These words were spoken...at the end of the Paschal meal which was followed by the events of those holy days during which confirmation was to be given once and for all of the fact that "God..., who is full of mercy, for his exceeding charity wherewith he loved us, even when we were dead in sins, hath quickened us together in Christ" (Eph. 2:4ff.).

The artistic formulation so rich in biblical references has already been commented on in the analysis of the theme. It remains to analyse the careful way in which it is written and the use of biblical texts.

The title of the Encyclical which refers to Eph. 2:4 makes the reader ask himself what St. Paul himself is saying in that verse in his epistle. The Apostle is describing (Eph. 2:1-9) the earlier way of life of the Christians who were formerly heathens or Jews when they were still under the influence of Satan and "by nature children of wrath" (Eph. 2:1-3). But then God's mercy and love brought about a change (cf. Eph. 2:4). This change says St. Paul is the Redemption as a passage from the death of sin to life. It happens with and in Christ by grace because of faith (Eph. 2:8).[6]

Starting the Encyclical with Eph. 2:4 does not mean that John Paul II intends to make the Apostle's teaching on the Redemption the theme of his Encyclical. If that were the case then it would be impossible for the Pope to continue teaching universal salvation in *Dives in Misericordia* as he did in *Redemptor Hominis*.

The careful way in which the text has been put together has the following structure: The Encyclical begins with "*Dives in Misericordia Deus*" from Ephesians (2:4) but does not quote directly (it changes the place of the word *Deus*) but then after the first few words interrupts this with the insertion of the theme and main points of the Encyclical before taking up the text again at the end of the paragraph and continuing to the end of the sentence.

It is clear then that Eph. 2:4 is only the framework for the formulation of the theme and main points. It is not Eph. 2:4 but the *insertion* which is more important. Starting the Encyclical with Eph. 2:4 is simply a means of giving the Encyclical its impressive title. The quotation is not exegetically developed. It is simply the point of departure for the formulation of the theme of how the Pope defines revelation. Thus the Pope's universal salvation thesis is put programmatically at the start of the Encyclical.

When the Pope finally comes back to Eph. 2:4ff. and quotes (almost) the whole sentence this is not in relation to what St. Paul is talking about in his epistle but rather the "events of those holy days" at the end of the Paschal meal,

> during which confirmation was to be given once and for all of the fact that "God..., who is full of mercy, for his exceeding charity wherewith he loved us, even when we were dead in sins, hath quickened us together in Christ" (Eph. 2:4ff.).

---

[6] Cf. Hans Conzelmann, *Der Brief an die Epheser* [*The Epistle to the Ephesians*] (Göttingen 1968), NTD VIII, pp. 64ff.

"The events of those holy days" are not, however, interpreted in the sense of St. Paul's teaching on the Redemption but rather according to the Pope's concept of revelation, that is, universal salvation (cf. *DiM* 7-8). The Encyclical never talks about those who are "by nature children of wrath" as St. Paul does (cf. Eph. 2:1-3) and who must first be redeemed from this state, he only talks about man "in the full dignity of his nature." Eph. 2:4 only gives the title. For the true meaning of the Encyclical it has no importance. It turns out to be just an artistic turn of style.[7]

1.3 Man is the Way of the Church

Just as in *Redemptor Hominis*, in *Dives in Misericordia* the Pope gives a picture of our present generation after the main theological part (*DiM* 10-12) in order to confront it with the Father's mercy in the mission of the Church (*DiM* 13-15). In this introduction he just defines the Church's central task in our needy times. He joins to the last sentence of the previous paragraph (*DiM* 1:2): "Man and man's lofty calling are revealed in Christ through the revelation of the mystery of the Father and His love" and continues (*DiM* 1:3):

> To turn oneself to this mystery is called for by the varied experiences of the Church and of contemporary man. It is also demanded by the pleas of many human hearts, their sufferings and hopes, their anxieties and expectations. While it is true that every individual human being is, as I said in my Encyclical *Redemptor Hominis*, the way for the Church, at the same time the Gospel and the whole of Tradition constantly show us that we must travel this way with every individual just as Christ traced it out by revealing in Himself the Father and His love (*GS* 22). In Jesus Christ, every path to

---

[7] Cf. Part II/1, pp. 46-49.

> man, as it has been assigned once and for all to the Church in the changing context of the times, is simultaneously an approach to the Father and His love. The Second Vatican Council has confirmed this truth for our time.

It is man whose deepest essence is revealed to man by Christ through the revelation of the Father and His love. The anthropocentrism of this way of looking at revelation determines the anthropocentric character of the Church's mission. The motto from *Redemptor Hominis* is also valid for *Dives in Misericordia*: "Man is the way in the Church."[8]

The Pope, however, goes beyond his first Encyclical when, calling on "the Gospel and the whole of Tradition" he says that this way has been traced out by Christ to the Church by "revealing in Himself the Father and His love" (*perinde ac designavit illam (viam) Christus, cum Patrem in se aperiret eiusque amorem*). What is compared, therefore, is the revelation of the Father in Christ Himself. That is why explains the Pope "that way" which leads from Christ to man is at the same time the way that leads "to the Father and His love" (*Quotiens igitur in Christo ad hominem via illa dirigitur, quae semel Ecclesiae commissa..., totiens Patri obviam proceditur et eius amori*). The English text of the Encyclical loses the sense of the Latin original. In the Latin it does not say that "every" but "that" (*illa*), that is, the previously mentioned way leads "in Christ to man" and at the same time to the Father also. "That way" is, however, so unusual that it needs some critical explanation.

Of course the Church, with every man, must go along the path shown by Christ. But Christ's words are not, "Man is the way" but "I am the way" (Jn. 14:6). That is why the Church's motto should be Christ—and not man!—is the way of the Church.[9] But this well known way of the *Imitation of Christ* is

---

[8] Cf. *Redemptor Hominis* 14.—Part II/1, pp. 187-191.

[9] *Ibid.*

not "that way" which the Encyclical is talking about. Here, and this sentence must be read twice, it is talking about a way by which *every man* in himself is to reveal the Father and His love "just as *Christ* in Himself revealed the Father and His love."

Christ could reveal the Father in Himself because He is the consubstantial Son of the Father. That is why He could also say, "Who sees me sees the Father." This unique revelation of the Father in Christ, which is because of the Incarnation of the *Logos*, is according to the text of the Encyclical the way shown by Christ which the Church with every man "has to" go.

We are faced with the question: how shall man, every man, "reveal the Father and His love in himself" as Christ "revealed the Father and His love in Himself"? And from this parallel comes quite logically the question: how shall man, every man, be able to say, as Christ said, "Who sees me sees the Father"? And the Church is supposed to awaken this consciousness of superhuman, divine dignity in every man!

How should this claim be understood? Is it at all possible to understand it or can it be understood?

The claim is not some careless statement but a well thought out consequence from the Pope's concept of revelation. From the anthropocentrism of the concept of revelation: "Christ announces man to man himself but he does this by means of the revelation of the Father and His love (cf. Jn. 17:6)" follows on from the anthropocentrism of the Church's mission according to the motto: "Man is the way in the Church."

For a man to be truly man for the Pope means "that the Son of God has (formally) united Himself by His Incarnation to every man."[10] By this man has "being in Christ" *a priori* within himself as his *raison d'être* for being man. "Christ's being" is like every man's "being in Christ" the "being the Son" of the

[10] Karol Wojtyla, *Sign of Contradiction*, p. 117-119.

Father. Just as the revelation of the Father in Christ is founded on the Incarnation of the Son so also the revelation of the Father in every man is founded on this very Incarnation of the Son in so far as the Son by His Incarnation unites Himself formally to every man and has communicated "being in Christ." But only when "Christ's being" is identical with the "being in Christ" of every man can one say that every man reveals the Father in himself as Christ does. The inevitable consequence of this parallel is: either man is God—like Jesus Christ or God is man—like Jesus Christ.

This problem isn't new. It was already dealt with in the first part when we analysed Cardinal Wojtyla's concept of revelation which essentially comes from Henri de Lubac.[11] Cardinal Siri draws the same conclusion from de Lubac's concept of revelation:

> Father de Lubac says that Christ, by revealing the Father and through being revealed by Him, reveals man to man himself in the end. What can this proposition mean? Either Christ is merely man or man is divine. Perhaps these conclusions are not so clearly expressed but they always lead to this conception of the supernatural which is implicitly present in human nature; from there the way is open, without wanting it consciously, to a fundamental anthropocentrism.[12]

The Pope does not exclude a "fundamental anthropocentrism" in his theology but rather takes it up resolutely and makes it the main point of his considerations (cf. *DiM* 1.4).

1.4 The organic link between anthropocentrism and theocentrism

This is what the Encyclical has to say about the relationship

---

[11] Part I, pp. 95-98.

[12] *Ibid.* p. 97.

between anthropocentrism and theocentrism in the Church's theology and mission (*DiM* 1.4):

> The more the Church's mission is centred upon man—the more it is, so to speak, anthropocentric—the more it must be confirmed and actualised theocentrically, that is to say, be directed in Jesus Christ to the Father. While the various currents of human thought both in the past and at present have tended and still tend to separate theocentrism and anthropocentrism, and even to set them in opposition to each other, the Church, following Christ seeks to link them up in human history, in a profound and organic way. And this is also one of the basic principles, perhaps the most important one, of the teaching of the last Council. Since, therefore, in the present phase of the Church's history we put before ourselves as our primary task the implementation of the doctrine of the great Council, we must act upon this principle with faith, with an open mind and with all our heart. In the Encyclical already referred to, I have tried to show that the deepening and the many-faceted enrichment of the Church's consciousness resulting from the Council must open our minds and our hearts more widely to Christ. Today I wish to say that openness to Christ, who as the Redeemer of the world fully "reveals man to himself," can only be achieved through an ever more mature reference to the Father and His love.

The text contains a thesis (a) and an *adhortatio* (b), which need to be gone into further.

a) The thesis is as follows: the more the Church's mission (*Ecclesiae opus*) is anthropocentric the more it must be confirmed theocentrically, that is to say, be directed in Jesus Christ to the Father (*theocentricale ratione: ordinandum nempe in Christi [sic] Iesu ad Patrem*).

The thesis is the last part of the development of the Encyclical's theme (*DiM* 1.1): from the Pope's concept of revelation (*DiM* 1.2) we get the anthropocentric motto for the Church's mission "man is the way in the Church" (cf. *DiM* 1.3). The Church's mission is once again concentrated anthropocentrically on man "in Christ" and at the same time directed towards the Father theocentrically (*DiM* 1.4).

The whole train of thought is nothing more than a logical application of the Pope's concept of revelation taken from *Gaudium et Spes* (22) on the Church's mission.

The anthropocentrism and theocentrism of this concept of revelation can be presented as follows:

"Christ announces man to himself." This revelation of man "in and through Christ" is obviously anthropocentric. It concentrates on man.

But the revelation of man occurs in and through Christ "by means of the revelation of the Father and His love": This historical revelation is directed theocentrically towards the Father "in and through Christ" in so far as it reveals the Father; and at the same time it concentrates on man anthropocentrically in so far as the revelation of the Father in and through Christ "reveals man to himself."

The "double revelation" in and through Christ is thus both anthropocentrically concentrated on man and theocentrically directed towards the Father, but *per se* and on the whole it has an "anthropocentric character" as Cardinal Wojtyla already showed in *Sign of Contradiction* (p. 120): it reveals "the mystery of man," it "deals therefore with man."[13]

From this anthropocentrism and theocentrism of the Encyclical's concept of revelation we get the mission of the Church which derives from it.

With the thesis of an organic link of anthropocentrism and theocentrism in revelation and the Church's mission the Pope comes to the heart of his whole theology: to his concept of revelation which affects everything else.

Thus we may understand the decisiveness with which he rejects all other ways of looking at revelation "past and present." And he justifies himself by calling on the highest of authori-

[13] Cf. Part I, pp. 110-123.

ties: Christ Himself, "perhaps the most important idea" of the last council and *Redemptor Hominis*. Apart from that he gives no other justification but just an *adhortatio* to willingly accept his thesis in faith.

There can, however, be no doubt that the Pope's concept of revelation is something completely new in the history of the Church's Magisterium. Nowhere in Church history do we find the Pope's conception of anthropocentrism and theocentrism in revelation because the Church's revelation principle is completely different. It was of course because biblical revelation and therefore also theology and the Church's mission are theocentrically directed. Theology is "teaching about God," and the Church's mission is to lead men to God.

In classical theology the material and formal object are both God Himself. It is the same for natural and supernatural theology. The classical definition is, "The formal object of natural theology is God as He is known by natural reason out of the Creation; The formal object of supernatural theology is God as He is known by faith from revelation."[14]

Biblical revelation and the Church's theology are not and essentially have never been anthropocentric but always theocentric. If words are to maintain their meaning then anthropocentric can only be theocentric at the same time if man is God or God is man. That is the case with Jesus Christ true God and true man. That is why a Christocentric theology is also theocentric, Christocentrism is also theocentrism because the man Jesus Christ is God Himself.

This thesis: anthropocentrism is the same as theocentrism leads inexorably to the conclusion that man is God or God is man. Then theology is anthropology and vice versa.

But that is not the Encyclical's thesis. It does not say, the more anthropocentric the Church's mission is the more it is theocentric, but the more it "must be theocentrically directed

[14] Ludwig Ott, *op. cit.* p. 1.

in Jesus Christ towards the Father." It is not claimed that they are the same but there is an inner, organic link between anthropocentrism and theocentrism. The organic link, however, is from "double revelation." But this is, in spite of all this talk about an organic link between anthropocentrism and theocentrism, on the whole concentrated on man. On the whole it has an "anthropocentric character."

One could object, in the Encyclical we are clearly talking about revelation and the Church's mission "in Christ." Mustn't a revelation like this which, in Christ, is directed anthropocentrically to man and theocentrically to the Father be called Christocentric?

That is, however, with the Encyclical's concept of revelation not possible. For the "double revelation" is also "in Christ" concentrated on man. The central point of reference of both means of revelation is man "in Christ." Christ Himself is the interpreter who "reveals man to man himself" and the historical revelation of the Father "in Christ" is what man announces. That is why even the theocentric revelation of the Father "in Christ" is not Christocentric but in the end also anthropocentric. The general anthropocentric character of the double revelation remains intact "*in Christus*" and determines the general character of the Church's mission which is as follows:

The Church's mission concentrates on man who is redeemed and justified *a priori*, has an inviolable dignity of being a Son and possesses "being in Christ" (=*a priori* revelation). This truth about man is revealed to man through and in Christ anthropocentrically. This is the case "theocentrically" once again "in Christ" by means of "the revelation of the Father and His love" (= *a posteriori* revelation). It is, however, clear that the historical revelation of the Father in Christ is in the end directed towards man anthropocentrically. That is why the general character of the Church's mission is concentrated on man, why "man is the way in the Church," why the Church's mission is "fundamentally anthropocentric."[15]

---

[15] Cf. Part I, pp. 110-123.

Thus we come back to the question once again (*cf.* above 1.3): what is the relationship between "Christ's being" and each human being's "Being in Christ" which is the *raison d'être* of man's being and where the Church's mission is concentrated? In the Encyclical's rigorous anthropocentrism the answer seems to be unavoidably: they are the same. The Son of God who united Himself formally by His Incarnation with every human being is thus the humano-divine principle of man's being.[16] *Dives in Misericordia* gives more details. For the Encyclical's theme is the "integrally existential reference" of man to God as Father without which man cannot be manifested "in the full dignity of his nature" (*DiM* 1.2). A reference which is revealed in the visible revelation of the Father in Christ.

b) In his *adhortatio* the Pope asks us in a general way to accept and make a reality in our lives the Council's basic idea of the link between anthropocentrism and theocentrism as it is presented in the Encyclical with faith and with an open mind.

The Encyclical names two fruits of that conciliar principle which have already been discussed in *Redemptor Hominis* (cf. *DiM* 1.4) and they are:

– the Church's new, full and universal self understanding (*RH* 11, 1). It claims that humanity as a whole is the invisible Church.[17]

– the second fruit is a new and more perfect knowledge of the mystery of the Redemption which Christianity received at the Second Vatican Council (cf. *RH* 11.3). Through the "opening up of the Church to Christ the Redeemer of the World" is said to have "fully revealed man to man" (*DiM* 1.4). And this full revelation is the knowledge of universal Redemption.[18]

---

[16] *Sign of Contradiction*, pp. 117ff.; cf. Part I, pp. 110ff.

[17] *Sign of Contradiction*, p. 101; Part II/1, pp. 141-149.

[18] Cf. Part II/1, pp. 181-187.

The declared aim of *Dives in Misericordia* is therefore to deepen and complete the new and more perfect knowledge from the Council of the Redeemer of all, by opening the consciousness to the universal Redeemer's Father who as love and mercy visibly appeared in Christ.

2. Plan of the Encyclical *

The sketch of the Encyclical divides it up materially. It is based on biblical revelation, first the Old and then the New Testament (Ch. II-V). Then there is a sketch of our present generation (Ch. VI) and of the divine mercy in the Church's mission for today (Ch. VII-VIII).

2.1 God's revelation in Creation and in Christ

The Encyclical is based on divine revelation (*DiM* 2.1):

> Although God "dwells in unapproachable light" (I Tim. 6:16), He speaks to man by means of the whole of the universe: "ever since the Creation of the world His invisible nature, namely, His eternal power and deity, has been clearly perceived in the things that have been made" (Rom. 1:20). This indirect and imperfect knowledge, achieved by the intellect seeking God by means of creatures through the visible world, falls short of "vision of the Father." "No one has ever seen God," writes St. John, in order to stress the truth that "the only Son, who is in the bosom of the Father, has made him known" (Jn. 1:18). This "making known" reveals God in the most profound mystery of His being, one and three, surrounded by "unapproachable light" (*Deum patefacit imperscrutabili in vitae ipsius mysterio—unum ac trinum—qui lucem habitat inaccessibilem.* I Tim. 6:16). Nevertheless, through this "making known" by Christ we know God above all in His relationship of love for man: in His "philanthropy" (Philanthrop'a Tit. 3:4). It is precisely here that "His invis-

* Article's title (2) in the English translation: "The Incarnation of Mercy."

> ible nature" becomes in a special way "visible," incomparably more visible than through all the other "things that have been made": it becomes visible in Christ and through Christ, through His actions and His words, and finally through His death on the cross and His resurrection.

The text reflects the classical teaching of natural and supernatural revelation and the knowledge of God. In this traditional beginning the Pope immediately goes to the heart of his Encyclical: to "seeing the Father" in the Son made man, to the visible revelation of God's "philanthropy" in Jesus Christ, in His deeds and words, in His death on the cross and His resurrection. Thus he has already communicated to the reader the development of the theme in the Life of Jesus Christ.

2.2 Divine mercy in the Old and New Testament

The Encyclical takes its teachings on the divine mercy from the sources of revelation of the Old and New Testament (*DiM* 2.2):

> In this way, in Christ and through Christ, God also becomes especially visible in His mercy: that is to say, there is emphasised that attribute of the divinity which the Old Testament, using various concepts and terms, already defined as "mercy." Christ confers on the whole of the Old Testament tradition about God's mercy a definitive meaning. Not only does He speak of it and explain it by the use of comparisons and parables, but above all He Himself makes it incarnate and personifies it. He Himself, in a certain sense, is mercy. To the person who sees it in Him—and finds it in Him—God becomes "visible" in a particular way as the Father "who is rich in mercy" (Eph. 2:4).

With this text biblical revelation and knowledge of God meet with the Encyclical's theme and main points and by this into the Pope's concept of revelation: Christ is the "embodiment of mercy," in His person God "becomes visible as Father who is full of mercy." In the last sentence which takes up Eph. 2:4 we have a similar formulation to the beginning of the Encyclical (cf. *DiM* 1.1).

At the same time the reader is made aware of the development of the theme: God's mercy in the Old Testament finds its definitive perfection in the New Testament.

2.3 Our age before God the Father of mercy and the Church's mission

After the main exegetical part the Pope gives a sketch taken from the pastoral constitution *Gaudium et Spes* on our times (*DiM* 2.3-2.4) and the Church's mission in the modern world (*DiM* 2.5-2.8). The Church must "think through" man's situation "in the light of the truth received from God" that is of divine mercy. Here is the most important paragraph (*DiM* 2.5):

> The truth, revealed in Christ, about God the "Father of mercies" (II Cor. 1:3), enables us to "see" Him as particularly close to man, especially when man is suffering, when he is under threat at the very heart of his existence and dignity. And this is why, in the situation of the Church and the world today, many individuals and groups guided by a lively sense of faith are turning, I would say almost spontaneously, to the mercy of God. They are certainly being moved to do this by Christ Himself, who through His Spirit works within human hearts. For the mystery of God the "Father of mercies" revealed by Christ becomes, in the context of today's threats to man, as it were a unique appeal addressed to the Church.

So ends the sketch or plan of the Encyclical.

The Pope sees the Holy Ghost at work in the hearts of many people of our time so that they turn spontaneously to the God of mercy. He sees there an urgent appeal to the Church of our age.

The Pope accepts this appeal. He makes the central theme of the Church's mission and his Encyclical the mystery of God as Father and His merciful love visibly revealed in Christ (*DiM* 2.6-2.8).

CHAPTER II

The Messiah Makes the Father Present as Mercy*

In the second chapter, using only one article (3) the Pope sketches the Messiah's mission and lays the foundation for the development of the theme in the Old and New Testament. (Ch. III-V).

3. The Messiah's mission**

The third article is like an overture to the Encyclical's theme. The *leitmotiv* clearly resounds in the careful way the Encyclical is constructed. Considering this construction as a whole is here the key to a better understanding of what is being said theologically. We shall give examples later.[1] That is why our commentary concentrates primarily on explaining the structure as a whole and how the text is put together: paragraph by paragraph the Encyclical gets closer to its object; at the same time each text from the New Testament is transposed into the Encyclical's theme and thus, with variations in how it is expressed, into the Pope's concept of revelation (*DiM* 3.1-3.5).

3.1 The first revelation of Jesus as Messiah in St. Luke (4:18ff.)

At the beginning we have Jesus' revelation of Himself as

---

* The chapter's title in the English translation is, "The Messianic Message."

** The article's title in the English translation is, "When Christ Began to Do and to Teach."

[1] Cf. above INTRODUCTION, 1. Presentation and Method (p. 17).

Messiah in the Synagogue at Nazareth (*DiM* 3.1):

> Before his own townspeople, in Nazareth, Christ refers to the words of the prophet Isaiah, "The Spirit of the Lord is upon me, because he has anointed me to preach good news to the poor. He has sent me to proclaim release to the captives and recovering of sight to the blind, to set at liberty those who are oppressed, to proclaim the acceptable year of the Lord" (Lk. 4:18ff.). These phrases, according to Luke, are His first messianic declaration which we see in the Gospel. By these actions and words Christ makes the Father present among men.

The words of the prophet Isaiah are the words of Scripture which the Pope uses to describe not only the "first" revelation but also the revelation of the Messiah full stop. Thus he has changed the Encyclical's whole way of looking at the revelation of the Messiah in the New Testament. At the same time this text receives its first and fundamental exegesis, "By these actions and words Christ makes the Father present among men." Thus the "first revelation of the Messiah" has already been adapted to the Encyclical's theme, and concept of revelation, even in its germinal form.

The Pope continues with his exegesis of Lk. 4:18ff. by interpreting the prophet's words (*DiM* 3.1):

> It is very significant that the people in question are especially poor, those without means of subsistence, those deprived of their freedom, the blind who cannot see the beauty of Creation, those living with broken hearts, or suffering from social injustice, and finally sinners. It is especially for these last that the Messiah becomes a particularly clear sign of God who is love, a sign of the Father. In this visible sign the people of our own time, just like the people then, can see the Father.

Thus the present revelation of the Messiah, concentrated on man's suffering, becomes part of the theme and the Encyclical's concept of revelation. The Messiah is a visible sign of God the Father who is love for all men.

3.2 The messengers from the Baptist and the testimony of Jesus

The Pope lets Jesus as it were ratify this interpreted revelation of the Messiah (*DiM* 3.2):

> It is significant that, when the messengers sent by John the Baptist came to Jesus to ask Him, "Are you he who is to come, or shall we look for another?," (Lk. 7:19) he answered by referring to the same testimony with which He had begun His teaching at Nazareth, "Go and tell John what it is that you have seen and heard: the blind receive their sight, the lame walk, lepers are cleansed, and the deaf hear, the dead are raised up, the poor have good news preached to them." He then ended with the words, "And blessed is he who takes no offence at me!" (Lk. 7:22ff).

With these words to the messengers from the Baptist Jesus Himself expressly confirms the first revelation of the Messiah and then underlines it by calling blessed all those who take no offence at "the visible sign of the Father."

3.3 Through Jesus' actions love is made present in our world

The first, interpreted and adapted revelation of the Messiah is now generalised by being extended to Jesus' general actions (*DiM* 3.3):

> Especially through His lifestyle and through His actions, Jesus revealed that love is present in the world in which we live—an effective love, a love that addresses itself to man and embraces everything that makes up his humanity. This love makes itself particularly noticed in contact with suffering, injustice and poverty—in contact with the whole historical "human condition," which in various ways manifests man's limitation and frailty, both physical and moral. It is precisely

the mode and sphere in which love manifests itself that in biblical language is called "mercy."

The first revelation of the Messiah is performed therefore in a general way by Jesus' lifestyle and actions. The conclusion is: the Messiah's effective love embraces in a loving and merciful way the whole historical "human condition," but especially the suffering "*conditio humana.*" Sin is not particularly mentioned in this conclusion. It is contained in "man's limitation and frailty, both physical and moral."

3.4 Jesus' effective love reveals the Father and makes Him present

By making in His life and actions the all embracing love towards man a reality, especially towards suffering man, the Messiah is the revelation of the Father and His love (*DiM* 3.4):

> Christ, then, reveals God who is Father, who is "love" (*Ideoque Christus Deum patefecit, qui Pater est, qui est "amor"*), as St. John expresses it in his first letter (I Jn. 4:8-16); Christ reveals God as "rich in mercy," as we read in St. Paul (Eph. 2:4). This truth is not just the subject of a teaching; it is a reality made present to us by Christ. Making the Father present as love and mercy is, in Christ's own consciousness, the fundamental touchstone of His mission as the Messiah; this is confirmed by the words that He uttered first in the synagogue at Nazareth and later in the presence of His disciples and of John the Baptist's messengers.

Thus Christ's whole life and actions as a realisation of the first revelation of the Messiah becomes once again part of the theme and hence of the Encyclical's concept of revelation. The Pope summarises the result of his consideration, which he lets Christ confirm, in one pregnant sentence:

> Making the Father present as love and mercy is, in Christ's

own consciousness, the fundamental touchstone of His mission as the Messiah.

Thus the circle of the revelation of the Father through Jesus' messianic actions is completed. This revelation becomes now the frame for Jesus' messianic words.

3.5 Jesus' teaching within the framework of the revelation of God as Father

We have not yet seen Jesus as a preacher. This aspect is now introduced, in the framework of the "fundamental realisation of the Messiah's mission" (*DiM* 3.5).

> On the basis of this way of manifesting the presence of God who is Father, love and mercy, Jesus makes mercy one of the principal themes of His preaching. As is His custom, He first teaches "in parables," since these express better the very essence of things. It is sufficient to recall the parable of the Prodigal Son (Lk. 15:11-32) or the parable of the Good Samaritan (Lk. 10:30-37) but also, by contrast, the parable of the merciless servant (Mt. 18:23-35). There are many passages in the teaching of Christ that manifest love-mercy under some ever-fresh aspect. We need only consider the Good Shepherd who goes in search of the lost sheep (Mt. 18:12-14; Lk. 15:3-7) or the woman who sweeps the house in search of the lost coin (Lk. 15:8-10).The Gospel writer who deals with these themes in Christ's teaching particularly is Luke, whose Gospel has earned the title of "the Gospel of mercy."

Thus the Pope transposes the preaching of Jesus as well—and so the whole public working of the Messiah—into the framework of the Encyclical's theme and principle of revelation. The parables mentioned certainly contain Jesus' Good News.[2] But what change do they undergo in the framework of

---

[2] Cf. Joachim Jeremias, *Die Gleichnisse Jesu* [*The Parables of Jesus*] (Zurich 1952), pp. 102ff.

the Encyclical's principle of revelation?[3]

3.6 The important problem: "The definition of mercy and love"

The main part of the Pope's consideration of Jesus' preaching is as follows:

> When one speaks of preaching, one encounters a problem of major importance with reference to the meaning of terms and the content of concepts, especially the content of the concept of "mercy" (in relationship to the concept of "love"). A grasp of the content of these concepts is the key to the understanding of the very reality of mercy. And this is what is most important for us. However, before devoting a further part of our considerations to this subject, that is to say, to establishing the meaning of the vocabulary and the content proper to the concept of "mercy," we must note that Christ, in revealing the love-mercy of God, at the same time demanded from people that they also should be guided in their lives by love and mercy. This requirement forms part of the very essence of the messianic message, and constitutes the heart of the Gospel ethos. The Teacher expresses this both through the medium of the commandment which He describes as "the greatest" (Mt. 22:38) and also in the form of a blessing, when in the Sermon on the Mount He proclaims, "Blessed are the merciful, for they shall obtain mercy." (Mt. 5:7).

According to this, the explanation of the terms mercy and love in Jesus' preaching is one of the main points of *Dives in Misericordia*. For an Encyclical such an aim is astonishing. The Pope gives as the main aim and the key to his Encyclical—with what theological justification?—something which is a matter for scientific exegesis and which can be looked up in

[3] See Ch. IV, the exegesis of the parable of the Prodigal Son.

any dictionary of the Old and New Testament. How far the Pope goes can be seen in his exegesis of the New Testament (Ch. 4-5).

The same may be said of the definition of mercy and love as the "centre of the evangelical ethos." Here one should remark on the well thought out formulation of the Encyclical's text that in Mt. 22:38 the "greatest" of the commandments is the love of God to which the second, the love of neighbour is likened (cf. Mt. 22:39). Christian charity is rooted in Christian love of God, that is, in the faith in Christ.

3.7 Review

The second chapter closes with a short review (*DiM* 3.7):

> In this way, the messianic message about mercy preserves a particular divine-human dimension. Christ, the very fulfilment of the messianic prophecy, by becoming the incarnation of the love that is manifested with particular force with regard to the suffering, the unfortunate and sinners, makes present and thus more fully reveals the Father, who is God "rich in mercy." At the same time, by becoming for people a model of merciful love for others, Christ proclaims by His actions even more than by His words that call to mercy which is one of the essential elements of the Gospel ethos. In this instance it is not just a case of fulfilling a commandment or an obligation of an ethical nature; it is also a case of satisfying a condition of major importance for God to reveal Himself in His mercy to man, "The merciful...shall obtain mercy."

In this way the Pope in a pregnant manner puts into his own words the messianic message and makes it fit in with the Encyclical's concept of revelation:

Christ Himself is the incarnation of mercy. In turning to the suffering, the miserable and the sinner He makes the Father present and thereby shows all the more perfectly the Father who is a God full of mercy (*praesentem adducit Patrem eoque modo plenius ostendit Patrem, qui Deus est "dives in mise-*

ricordia").

Stylistically brilliant the overture of the Encyclical begins and ends with the title and *leitmotiv* "*dives in misericordia.*"

The messianic message of divine mercy is completed by the Christian ethos of mercy.

Doubtlessly Christ is the incarnation of mercy. Doubtlessly Christ is *the* "Model" of the "Christian ethos." The question is whether the Encyclical's main aim, the understanding of the definitions of mercy and love (cf. *DiM* 3.6) can be reconciled with the Gospel or whether preconceptions about revelation will change it into something else. In the end the question is whether the Messiah of the Encyclical is the same Christ from the Gospel and the Christian ethos of the Encyclical the same as that of the New Testament.

3.8 Critical review of chapter II

The critical review of the commentary of the whole of the second chapter is first of all an admiration for the magnificent composition, the exposition centred on the theme and the compressed reflection of the Messiah's mission. The commentary's praise of the religious depth seems understandable. Even if there is in Chapter II only an introductory sketch of the whole Encyclical, nonetheless the contours of the whole conception are clearly recognisable.

Starting from St. Luke's Gospel, what happens in Nazareth right at the beginning of Jesus' public ministry has a typical significance just as the words of the prophet quoted by Him have a central meaning.

In the Encyclical's structure "Jesus' first revelation as Messiah" according to St. Luke (4:18ff.) is the basis and framework for the presentation of the mission and the activity of the Messiah. The theological statement and the composition of the whole text form a single unity. The former may therefore be drawn out of the formation of the latter as a whole.

In the original context of the Old Testament the words of the prophet Isaiah announce a change for the better in the fortunes of the misery stricken Israelites returning from exile: a year of God's grace. By applying (and slightly changing) the prophet's words to Himself, Jesus says to his neighbours: the time of salvation is here, for the Messiah is here! You are eyewitnesses that this scripture has been fulfilled.[4]

"Jesus' first revelation as Messiah" is therefore not simply the "revelation of the Father," but of the Messiah.

In St. Luke's Gospel "Jesus' first revelation as Messiah" is directly and indissolubly linked to this claim to be the Messiah. This challenge to believe in His person enrages the community. They refuse faith and try to kill Jesus. Already in these events in St. Luke's Gospel we see what the Messiah can expect in His public mission from His people. His messianic mission ends on Calvary.

The Encyclical mentions none of this.

Also in the Gospel "Jesus' first revelation as Messiah" in Nazareth is the announcement of His messianic programme. His miraculous cures are proof of the fulfilment of the prophet Isaiah's words. Just as His "first revelation as Messiah" is directly and indissolubly linked to the challenge of the faith in His person so are His messianic actions. All of Jesus' public ministry takes place in the framework of the challenge to believe. It is because of this claim that His messianic actions become a stumbling block.

In the New Testament "Jesus' first revelation as Messiah" and His messianic actions are in the context of the preaching of the Kingdom of God. The Son of God came down from Heaven and became man "*propter nos homines.*" Full of mercy and healing, He also considered every suffering of man. But all this was in the end "*propter nostram salutem*" and for our

---

4 Cf. Karl Heinrich Rengstorf, *Das Evangelium nach Lukas* [*The Gospel According to St. Luke*] (Göttingen 1967), NTD III, pp. 67ff.—Karl Staab, *Das Evangelium nach Lukas* (Würzburg 1956, Echter-Bibel), pp. 37ff.—Joachim Jeremias, *Jesu Verheißung für die Völker* [*Jesus' Promise for the Nations*] (Stuttgart 1956), pp. 37ff.

"eternal" salvation.

In the Encyclical "Jesus' first revelation as Messiah" and His messianic actions appear without any challenge to believe. They are completely divorced from their biblical context of the announcement of the Kingdom of God. They are thus one-sidedly applied to the removal of earthly suffering and interpreted, ratified and generalised in this way. The framework of the messianic mission is the healing of all human suffering, a universal love of man. The Messiah's working did not have for its aim the restoration of a state of paradise here on earth to the chagrin of all Israel's expectations.

Coupled with this reduction of the biblical revelation of the Messiah to the simply human is the transposition of a few selected New Testament texts in a form distorted to fit the Encyclical's theme and view of revelation: In the general love of man for man the all merciful love of the Father is revealed. This distorted form determines the central message of the New Testament. This can clearly be seen in the Encyclical's two main theses which we have looked at:

The first main thesis describes summarily "how" the Messiah's "active love" works (cf. 3.3-4):

> According to this Jesus, through His life and actions revealed and made present the effect of love in our world. His effective love embraces the whole of historical humanity, quite simply the *conditio humana*, especially its limitations and weakness. By doing this He revealed God who is Father—who is "love."

The second main thesis describes summarily the aim or the reason why of the Messiah's mission (*DiM* 3.4):

> To make present the Father as love and mercy is for (Christ) the fundamental actualisation of His mission as Messiah (cf. *DiM* 3.4)

Both main theses seem at first sight to reflect the spirit of the New Testament. This first impression changes when one realises that in the presentation of the Messiah's mission in the Encyclical it is a question of the *Redeemer's* mission and therefore the Pope's soteriology is in play. The special character of the two theses is best seen in what they *do not* say.

In the general characterisation of the Messiah's all embracing love sin is not mentioned by name (cf. *DiM* 3.3). It is implied in man's "moral limitations." In other places sinners are mentioned in the same breath as the suffering and the unhappy (cf. *DiM* 3.1; 3.7).

Sin is, however, decisive in the "*conditio humana*" for the Messiah of the New Testament. Sin is not on the same plane as other evils in this world. It is the root of all evils in the sense of the "radical" separation of man from God that is Original Sin.[5]

In the New Testament the Messiah is above all the sinner's Redeemer. In His redeeming love He does not simply embrace everything human, rather His redeeming love is there to redeem man: to convert the sinner, to reconcile him with God. This Messiah is not so much interested in the temporal life as in the eternal. "What doth it profit a man if he gain the whole world but lose his soul?" (Mt. 16:26). Even when Christ embraces the whole of man's suffering with His merciful love, He is more interested in the Faith and the eternal salvation of man rather than just a cure. Indeed in Nazareth He could perform no miracles because He found no faith there (cf. Mk. 6:5). At any rate the Messiah reveals in the Gospel "how" His effective love works by always making clear the relationship with faith and eternal life. This is particularly evident in the cure of the paralytic (Mk. 2:1-12). This "how" was not simply an embracing of what is involved in making man human. It goes much deeper. It is a question of the relationship of man to God which has been fundamentally destroyed by Original

---

[5] Cf. Rom. 3:9ff.; 5:1ff.

Sin. To heal this relationship and to redeem and reconcile man who has been separated from God through His blood is the "fundamental actualisation of the Messiah's mission" in the New Testament.

The same goes for the Encyclical's second main thesis. Of course the Messiah made the love of the Father visible and present in His mission. But the "fundamental actualisation of Christ's mission as Messiah" is the Redemption of man which the Saviour wrought to the glory of God and the salvation of man. Why is it precisely this central dogma, the Son of God was made man in order to redeem us from sin through His cross, which is missing in the magnificent overture of the Pope's teaching on Redemption?[6]

The reason is clear: the Encyclical's soteriology is based on the "double revelation" principle. If all men from the beginning to the end of the world have already been redeemed and justified by the Cross of Christ[7] then the work of man's Redemption has already essentially been carried out. It then remains for the "fundamental actualisation of the Messiah's mission" only to reveal "the Father as love and mercy" and "make Him present" in our world. Then the Messiah in His loving turning towards the suffering left over in this world is just "a sign of the Father who is love and mercy."

In the Encyclical the active love of the Messiah is infinitely open to the purely human but there is absolutely no mention of man's absolute need for Redemption from Original Sin nor of the necessity of faith and baptism for salvation. What is missing is precisely the essential and specific redeeming love of Christ.

---

[6] Cf. Ludwig Ott, *Fundamentals of Catholic Dogma,* trans. Patrick Lynch (Herder Book, St. Louis, 1954), p. 175.

[7] Karol Wojtyla, *Sign of Contradiction*, p.101.

CHAPTER III

The Old Testament

In the third chapter (art. 4) we have the exegetical development of the theme. The main aim is to explain the word "mercy" and its relation to love and justice.

The Pope begins with the Old Testament as a background "that the mercy revealed by Christ may shine forth more clearly" (*DiM* 4.1).

4. God's mercy in the history of Israel *

In the commentary on this article we shall not give lengthy quotations from the Encyclical but rather present a short essay in which the most important points of the Pope's train of thought will be cited literally.

4.1 The experience of mercy in the history of a frequently-broken covenant

When Christ revealed God's mercy by word and deed, He

> addressed Himself to people who not only knew the concept of mercy, but who also, as the People of God of the Old Covenant, had drawn from their age-long history a special experience of the mercy of God (*DiM* 4.1).

Israel's history is the history of a covenant with God, "a

* The English translation has the following title for the whole article, "The Concept of 'Mercy' in the Old Testament" but no titles for the sub-articles.

covenant which is often broken." When Israel became aware of her unfaithfulness she called on the mercy of God. This we read in the books of the Old Testament (*DiM* 4.2).

The prophets announce God's mercy with the chosen people using images of tender love (*DiM* 4.3):

> The Lord loves Israel with the love of a special choosing, much like the love of a spouse, and for this reason He pardons its sins and even its infidelities and betrayals. When He finds repentance and true conversion, He brings His people back to grace. In the preaching of the prophets, mercy signifies a special power of love, which prevails over the sin and infidelity of the chosen people.

Mercy does not just affect God's relationship with His people but also with every member of this people. In every need the sons and daughters of Israel turn to the Lord and call upon His mercy. Divine mercy embraces "both physical evil and moral evil namely sin" (*DiM* 4.4).

4.2 Already in the beginning there is a fundamental experience of mercy

Israel experienced God's mercy especially in her history. There is a fundamental experience of divine mercy right at the beginning (*DiM* 4.5):

> The Lord saw the affliction of His people reduced to slavery, heard their cry, knew their sufferings and decided to deliver them. In this act of salvation by the Lord, the prophet perceived his love and compassion (cf. Is. 63:9).This is precisely the grounds upon which the people and each of its members based their certainty of the mercy of God, which can be invoked whenever tragedy strikes.

Later on, regarding the wretchedness of the enslaved people, the Pope mentions (*DiM* 4.6): "Added to this is the fact that sin too constitutes man's misery."

Man's wretchedness in sin appears almost like an added "ingredient" to man's general misery. In the Old Testament, however, it is the central point of the relationship of God with Israel. The history of the covenant is the history of the First Commandment.[1]

In its substance the misery of sin is determined by the Encyclical as the falling away from the God of the Covenant and it is also given some consideration: it is seen in the apostate people's dance around the golden calf.

God's reaction to this central breach of the covenant is divine mercy. God's wrath is not mentioned (*DiM* 4.6):

> The Lord Himself triumphed over this act of breaking the covenant when He solemnly declared to Moses that He was a "God merciful and gracious, slow to anger, and abounding in steadfast love and faithfulness" (Ex. 34:6).

From this source Israel's piety received an unshakeable trust in God's mercy (4.6):

> It is in this central revelation that the chosen people, and each of its members, will find, every time that they have sinned, the strength and the motive for turning to the Lord to remind Him of exactly what He had revealed about Himself and to beseech His forgiveness.

The revelation of God's mercy with His people shows from the beginning all types of the Lord's love for His own (*DiM* 4.7):

> He is their Father (cf. Is. 63:16) for Israel is His firstborn son (cf. Ex. 4:22); the Lord is also the bridegroom of her whose new name the prophet proclaims, "*Ruhamah*," "Beloved" or "she has obtained pity" (Hos. 2:3).

---

1 Cf. Gerhard v. Rad, *Theologie des Alten Testamentes* [*Theology of the Old Testament*] (Munich 1962, 5th edition), pp. 216ff.

God's generous love for His people that causes Him always to forget His wrath makes the Psalmist praise His love, His tenderness, His mercy and His faithfulness (*DiM* 4.8).

What does all this mean for the biblical conception of God and of Israel's piety? The answer is (*DiM* 4.9):

> From all this it follows that mercy does not pertain only to the notion of God, but it is something that characterises the life of the whole people of Israel and each of its sons and daughters: mercy is the content of intimacy with their Lord, the content of their dialogue with Him.

The aim of the Pope's exegesis is to draw "especially the definition of mercy" out of the history of the covenant with Israel. About this he says (*DiM* 4.9):

> It may be difficult to find in these books a purely theoretical answer to the question of what mercy is in itself. Nevertheless, the terminology that is used is in itself able to tell us much about this subject.

4.3 The definition of mercy in Israel's history

In one of the many pages of notes (no. 52) the Encyclical gives in some detail an exegetical definition as one might read in a good dictionary.[2] In the Encyclical's text there is the following review (*DiM* 4.10):

In order to express the experience of mercy, the Old Testament uses various words which have different meanings but which as it were "all converge from different directions on one single fundamental content." This fundamental content is described in the following way (*DiM* 4.10):

> The Old Testament encourages people suffering from mis-

[2] E.g. Kittel's [*Theological Dictionary of the New Testament*], II, 474-483.

> fortune, especially those weighed down by sin—as also the whole of Israel, which had entered into the covenant with God—to appeal for mercy, and enables them to count upon it: it reminds them of His mercy in times of failure and loss of trust. Subsequently, the Old Testament gives thanks and glory for mercy every time that mercy is made manifest in the life of the people or in the lives of individuals.

In this way "mercy is in a certain sense contrasted with God's justice," and in many cases is shown to be not only stronger but also more profound because love is primary and fundamental. The relationship between justice and mercy in God is said to have its foundation in "God's relations with man and the world" thus finally in "the very mystery of Creation." That is why we must go back to "the beginning" (*DiM* 4.11).[3]

By going back to the "mystery of Creation" the Pope makes his presentation of the Old Testament as a whole flow into the beginning of his theology on the covenant. In this way he anchors the history of the covenant in the act of Creation, in order to interpret it in a new way (cf. *DiM* 4.12).

4.4 The covenant with man at the beginning of Creation

While he was still Cardinal Wojtyla, John Paul II stressed that human history can only really be under stood from the beginning of the Creation.[4] In the Encyclical he presents this view as follows (*DiM* 4.12):

> Connected with the mystery of Creation is the mystery of the election, which in a special way shaped the history of the people whose spiritual father is Abraham by virtue of his faith. Nevertheless, through this people which journeys forward through the history both of the Old Covenant and of the New, that mystery of election refers to every man and woman,

---

[3] Cf. Part II/1, pp. 24-32; 118-131.

[4] Cf. Karol Wojtyla, *Sign of Contradiction*, pp. 19ff.

to the whole great human family.

"I have loved you with an everlasting love, therefore I have continued my faithfulness to you" (Jer. 31:3). "For the mountains may depart...my steadfast love shall not depart from you, and my covenant of peace shall not be removed" (Is. 54:10). This truth, once proclaimed to Israel, involves a perspective of the whole history of man, a perspective both temporal and eschatological (Jn. 4:2.11 *etc.*). Christ reveals the Father within the framework of the same perspective and on ground already prepared, as many pages of the Old Testament writings demonstrate. At the end of this revelation, on the night before He dies, He says to the apostle Philip these memorable words, "Have I been with you so long, and yet you do not know me...? He who has seen me has seen the Father" (Jn. 14:9).

The text is a perfect formulation in a complete chain of thought whose logic can be seen when what is said in each sentence is interpreted in the sense of the papal theology and then reveiwed in the light of traditional teaching:

There is only one mention of the mystery of Creation in the first sentence, "Connected with the mystery of Creation is the mystery of the election." This sentence which is so decisive for the understanding of the whole passage seems to be a theologically obvious thing to say. It is, however, as it stands a completely neutral thing and open to any interpretation. In the Encyclical it is obviously to be understood in the sense of the Pope's theology of the covenant and then it has a very clear meaning: By being created man is chosen. The "Mystery of election" means that God by creating Adam *actu uno* made a covenant of grace with him, *i.e.,* with every man with humanity. This *ab origine* covenant of grace is indissoluble and inviolable. The mystery of election is thus the mystery of the giving of grace to everyone.[5]

---

5 Cf. The Pope's theology of the covenant in Part II/1, pp. 24-32 & pp. 118ff.

From this starting point the presentation of the quoted text is absolutely consistent: The *per se* universal mystery of the election of all men affected the history of the chosen people only "in a special way." This biblical term "election" is the verbal bridge which joins the irrevocable general giving of grace to all men *ab origine* with the history of the chosen people whose Father because of his Faith is Abraham.

If the history of the chosen people is the special expression or the particular sign of the election of the whole of humanity then through this people the mystery of universal salvation extends through the history of the Old and the New Testament to every individual man, to the whole vast family of man (*At tamen per hunc ipsum populum...refertur mysterium electionis istud ad unumquemque hominem et immensam cunctam hominum familiam*). In the quoted text God's oath of loyalty and love quite consistently is not just made with reference to Israel but also with reference to the irrevocable covenant of grace with humanity. Then this truth once announced to Israel (universal election or giving of grace to all) bears in actual fact a perspective both temporal and eschatological of all humanity in itself. In *this* perspective Christ is supposed to have revealed the Father to the listeners of His people prepared in this way. The main point of this revelation of God the Father rich in mercy is said to be contained in Christ's words, "He who has seen me has seen the Father" (Jn. 14:8). With the last sentence the Pope joins up with the beginning of the Encyclical (*DiM* 1.1), which contains the thesis of universal salvation *in nuce*.

One should remark with reference to the Pope's view of the situation the traditional teaching of the Church:

It is also possible to say in the sense of traditional teaching that the mystery of Creation is linked with the mystery of election. Adam began his existence with *iustitia originalis*. But the covenant of grace with Adam was not indissoluble, it was broken. The grace of original justice was lost by our first parents. In Scripture there is no unbroken or unbreakable covenant of Grace *ab origine* between God and man. Basically this is enough to reject the Encyclical's theology of the Covenant which is simply a consistent explanation of the idea of an unbreakable covenant of grace *ab origine.*

Since, after Original Sin, there has never been such an unbreakable covenant of grace between God and man it also cannot have affected the history of that people "whose Father because of his Faith is Abraham."

That is why Israel's path in the Faith of Abraham does not lead through the New Testament. Rather Israel's path in the Faith of Abraham leads directly to Christ and because of the Faith in Christ to the New Israel, the Church (cf. Rom. 3:21-4:25). The Old Testament has its fulfilment and therefore its end in the New (Rom. 10:4).

That is why the giving of grace to everyone *ab origine* is in no way the perspective of the "writings of the Old Testament," neither of Christ's listeners, neither of Christ's preaching. Christ also did not reveal the Father in this perspective.

Even in the early Church it was disputed whether the heathen could receive baptism without the Law.

The result of our analysis is that the Encyclical's theme leads to a picture of God in the Old Testament whose only quality is mercy and where all other ways of revealing God's nature are left out. By taking divine mercy in the Old Testament back to the mystery of Creation and an absolute universal election, the Encyclical comes to a completely new interpretation of the whole of the history of revelation and salvation in the Old Testament from the point of view of universal salvation. This new interpretation becomes clear in the last paragraph of the quoted text. The subtle change of meaning of what the Old Testament says is hardly perceptible before that because the history of the covenant in general seems unchanged and only at the end, by the axiom of universal salvation since the Creation of man, does it receive a new more universal interpretation.

CHAPTER IV

The New Testament:*

The Parable of the Prodigal Son

The fourth chapter (art. 5 & 6) deals with God's mercy in Christ's teaching (cf. above 3.5). The paradigm is the parable of the Prodigal Son (Lk. 15:11-32).

It is the only parable which is presented and interpreted in the "Trinitarian Trilogy." From this impressive parable the Pope draws as exemplary of Christ's teaching the main thrust of his theology. The aim of his exegesis is to go from the biblical parable to the heart of the truth of revelation of divine mercy in the New Testament, not so much by using terminology as analogy (cf. *DiM* 5.2).

5. The figure of the Prodigal Son**

After a short bridge from the Old to the New Testament (*DiM* 5.1-2) the Pope presents the figure first of the Prodigal Son (*DiM* 5.3-6), then that of the father (*DiM* 6). The older son receives no detailed attention (cf. *DiM* 6.1 & 2).

5.1 Echo of the Old Testament in the New

The Encyclical begins with the canticles at the beginning of St. Luke's Gospel (*DiM* 5.1):

> At the very beginning of the New Testament, two voices

* Chapter title in the English translation only, "Parable of the Prodigal Son."

** Article title in the English translation, "An Analogy."

> resound in St. Luke's Gospel in unique harmony concerning the mercy of God, a harmony which forcefully echoes the whole Old Testament tradition. They express the semantic elements linked to the differentiated terminology in the ancient books. Mary, entering the house of Zechariah, magnifies the Lord with all her soul for "his mercy," which "from generation to generation" is bestowed upon them that fear Him. A little later, as she recalls the election of Israel, she proclaims the mercy which He who has chosen her holds "in remembrance" from all time. Afterwards, in the same house, when John the Baptist is born, his father Zechariah blesses the God of Israel and glorifies Him for performing the mercy promised to our fathers and for remembering His holy covenant.

After this bridge from the Old Testament to the New the Encyclical comes to speak of Christ Himself. The praise of Mary, "His mercy is from generation to generation" (Lk. 1:50), is like a *leitmotiv* throughout the whole Encyclical.

5.2 Parable of divine mercy

"In the teaching of Christ Himself," it continues (*DiM* 5.2),

> this image inherited from the Old Testament becomes at the same time simpler and more profound. This is perhaps most evident in the parable of the Prodigal Son (Lk. 15:11-32). Although the word "mercy" does not appear, it nevertheless expresses the essence of the divine mercy in a particularly clear way. This is due not so much to the terminology, as in the Old Testament books, as to the analogy that enables us to understand more fully the mystery of mercy, as a profound drama played out between the father's love and prodigality and sin of the son.

Thus the Pope draws the reader's attention to the parable of the Prodigal Son and at the same time the crux of his own exegesis: analogy.

It is only when it is closely examined that the Encyclical's deliberate train of thought is made clear. In order to leave the papal exegesis as much as possible untouched we shall keep our commentary to just critical remarks and bring out the essential points in this train of thought.

5.3 The Prodigal Son: Man of every period

The Encyclical assumes the reader knows the parable and so begins with its detailed exegesis (*DiM* 5.3):

> That son who receives from the father the portion of the inheritance that is due to him and leaves home to squander it in a far country "in loose living," in a certain sense is the man of every period, beginning with the one who was the first to lose the inheritance of grace and original justice. The analogy at this point is very wide-ranging. The parable indirectly touches upon every breach of the covenant of love, every loss of grace, every sin. In this analogy there is less emphasis than in the prophetic tradition of the unfaithfulness of the whole people of Israel, although the analogy of the Prodigal Son may extend to this also. "When he had spent everything," the son "began to be in need," especially as "a great famine arose in that country" to which he had gone after leaving his father's house. And in this situation "he would gladly have fed on" anything, even "the husks of swine," the swine that he herded for "one of the citizens of that country." But even this was refused him.

This presentation of the Prodigal Son is an essay on the biblical parable which needs no commentary. What we should notice is the analogy which has been put into this essay.

– the Prodigal Son is "in a certain sense is the man of every period, beginning with the one who was the first to to lose the inheritance of grace and original justice."

– The other analogies: every breach of the covenant of love, every loss of grace, every sin, the unfaithfulness of the whole people of Israel can be passed over since they play no part in the interpretation of the parable.

5.4 The analogy turns towards man's interior

The Encyclical turns now to the interior life of the Prodigal Son (*DiM* 5.4):

> The analogy turns clearly towards man's interior. The inheritance that the son had received from his father was a quantity of material goods, but more important than these goods was his dignity as a son in his father's house. The situation in which he found himself when he lost the material goods should have made him aware of the loss of that dignity. He had not thought about it previously, when he had asked his father to give him the part of the inheritance that was due to him, in order to go away. He seems not to be conscious of it even now, when he says to himself, "how many of my father's hired servants have bread enough and to spare, but I perish here with hunger." [1] He measures himself by the standard of the goods that he has lost, that he no longer "possesses," while the hired servants of his father's house "possess" them. These words express above all his attitude to material goods; nevertheless, under their surface is concealed the tragedy of lost dignity, the awareness of squandered sonship.

The Encyclical shows, as does the biblical parable, first of all the external misery of the Prodigal Son out of which matures the decision to return home. What is special about this description is that it concentrates on the material view of the son and the exegesis of his words. Thus the Pope says: from his words we can see that he is interested in external goods. But this veneer hides the "drama of lost dignity, the awareness of squandered sonship."

The clear statement of the son's "lost dignity" in his father's house and the "squandered sonship" seem to be in open contradiction to the thesis of universal salvation.[2]

---

1 In comparison to the Latin text the English translation starts no new paragraph here. We follow the English translation.

2 Cf. the clear statement of universal salvation in *Redemptor Hominis* 13.3; Part I, pp. 78ff., Part II/1, pp. 181ff.

5.5 The Prodigal Son's decision to return home

The Prodigal Son's decision to return home which comes from material wretchedness is interpreted as follows (*DiM* 5.5):

> It is at this point that he makes the decision, "I will arise and go to my father, and I will say to him, 'Father, I have sinned against heaven and before you; I am no longer worthy to be called your son. Treat me as one of your hired servants'" (Lk. 15:18ff.). These are words that reveal more deeply the essential problem. Through the complex material situation in which the Prodigal Son found himself because of his folly, because of sin, the sense of lost dignity had matured. When he decides to return to his father's house, to ask his father to be received—no longer by virtue of his right as a son, but as an employee—at first sight he seems to be acting by reason of the hunger and poverty that he had fallen into; this motive, however, is permeated by an awareness of a deeper loss: to be a hired servant in his own father's house is certainly a great humiliation and source of shame. Nevertheless, the Prodigal Son is ready to undergo that humiliation and shame. He realises that he no longer has any right except to be an employee in his father's house. His decision is taken in full consciousness of what he has deserved and of what he can still have a right to in accordance with the norms of justice. Precisely this reasoning demonstrates that, at the centre of the Prodigal Son's consciousness, the sense of lost dignity is emerging, the sense of that dignity that springs from the relationship of the son with the father. And it is with this decision that he sets out.

According to this the Prodigal Son's words bring the essential problem into view. This is as follows: out of material need matures the sense of lost dignity of sonship until the clear knowledge: I have lost dignity of being a son which came from the relationship of being my father's son, but according to the norms of justice I still have the right to be a hired servant even if this state of being a servant in my father's house is for me "a humiliation and shame."

This consideration is the substance of the decision which makes the Prodigal Son return to his father.

5.6 The permanence of being a son

The Prodigal Son's right according to the "norms of justice" is the Pope's point of departure whence he asks quite generally about the relationship between justice and merciful love in Jesus' parable (*DiM* 5.6):

> In the parable of the Prodigal Son, the term "justice" is not used even once; just as in the original text the term "mercy" is not used either. Nevertheless, the relationship between justice and love, that is manifested as mercy, is inscribed with great exactness in the content of the Gospel parable. It becomes more evident that love is transformed into mercy when it is necessary to go beyond the precise norm of justice—precise and often too narrow. The Prodigal Son, having wasted the property he received from his father, deserves—after his return—to earn his living by working in his father's house as a hired servant and possibly, little by little, to build up a certain provision of material goods, though perhaps never as much as the amount he had squandered. This would be demanded by the order of justice, especially as the son had not only squandered the part of the inheritance belonging to him but had also hurt and offended his father by his whole conduct. Since this conduct had in his own eyes deprived him of his dignity as a son, it could not be a matter of indifference to his father. It was bound to make him suffer. It was also bound to implicate him in some way. And yet, after all, it was his own son who was involved, and such a relationship could never be altered or destroyed by any sort of behaviour (*Agitur ad extremum tamen de proprio filio; neque illa necessitas auferri valuit nec qualibuscumque actibus dissolvi*). The Prodigal Son is aware of this and it is precisely this awareness that shows him clearly the dignity which he has lost and which makes him honestly evaluate the position that he could still expect in his father's house.

The word justice does not occur in the biblical parable because there is no claim to rights on the part of the returned son and thus no problem of the relationship between justice and merciful love. This problem is invented by the Pope and inserted into St. Luke's Gospel. It can be summarised thus:

The relationship between justice and mercy exists concretely in the rights that remain for the returning son and the father rich in mercy.

What is special in this relationship is the familial relationship: the son has "hurt and offended" his father by his behaviour but son remains son and father remains father.

It is a convincing argument which every father of a wayward son can understand as can every wayward son, the prodigal included.

That is why it is "precisely this knowledge"—as it says in the text—which makes the Prodigal Son "clearly recognise the dignity which he has lost and honestly evaluate the position that he could still expect in his father's house." It is also "precisely this knowledge" which makes the son return home.

We can give the substance of the Pope's argumentation in three sentences which are not completely incontrovertible: The Prodigal Son has "squandered his sonship" (*filietatis dissipatae*) and lost his dignity of being a son. It is now left him according to justice a right to be a hired labourer in his father's house. However, the bond of blood between the father and the son could not be put aside nor dissolved.

6. The figure of the father in the parable*

Up to now the Pope has described the Prodigal Son, now he describes the father.

6.1 The divine mercy is revealed in the father

The Pope continues with his exegesis of the parable (*DiM*

* Article title in the English translation, "Particular Concentration on Human Dignity."

6.1):

> This exact picture of the Prodigal Son's state of mind enables us to understand exactly what the mercy of God consists in. There is no doubt that in this simple but penetrating analogy the figure of the father reveals to us God as Father. The conduct of the father in the parable and his whole behaviour, which manifests his internal attitude, enables us to rediscover the individual threads of the Old Testament vision of mercy in a synthesis which is totally new, full of simplicity and depth. The father of the Prodigal Son is faithful to his fatherhood, faithful to the love that he had always lavished on his son. This fidelity is expressed in the parable not only by his immediate readiness to welcome him home when he returns after having squandered his inheritance; it is expressed even more fully by that joy, that merrymaking for the squanderer after his return, merrymaking which is so generous that it provokes the opposition and hatred of the elder brother, who had never gone far away from his father and had never abandoned the home.

The "state of mind" of the son corresponds with the "internal attitude" of the father. And this "internal attitude" of the father reveals the divine mercy. Thus the relationship of mercy and justice is quite concretely defined, as the Pope sees it, and written with great exactness into the biblical parable.

The quoted text has two very important things to say about the father:

– The figure of the father in the parable is an analogy of "God the Father." In this God's mercy as it was seen in the Old Testament is seen "in a synthesis which is totally new, full of simplicity and depth."

– The synthesis is the fatherly love of God. The father of the Prodigal Son is true to himself: to his fatherhood and love which he had given to his son from always.

The proof for the faithfulness of the father to himself is the readiness with which he receives his son when he returns home and the inexpressible joy with which he covers the squanderer with gifts. This provokes the opposition and envy of his elder son.

6.2 The father's faithfulness to himself

The father's faithfulness to himself is described in the Encyclical with images taken from the parable (*DiM* 6.2):

> The father's fidelity to himself—a trait already known by the Old Testament term "hesed"—is at the same time expressed in a manner particularly charged with affection. We read, in fact, that when the father saw the Prodigal Son returning home "he had compassion, ran to meet him, threw his arms around his neck and kissed him" (Lk. 15:20). He certainly does this under the influence of a deep affection, and this also explains his generosity towards his son, that generosity which so angers the elder son.

This confirms what has already been said: the behaviour of the father is the visible sign that "the father of the Prodigal Son is true to himself: to his fatherhood and love which he had given to his son from always."

The Pope develops this consistently by asking after the deeper reasons for it (*DiM* 6.2):

> Nevertheless, the causes of this emotion are to be sought at a deeper level. Notice, the father is aware that a fundamental good has been saved: the good of his son's humanity. Although the son has squandered the inheritance, nevertheless his humanity is saved. Indeed, it has been, in a way, found again. The father's words to the elder son reveal this, "It was fitting to make merry and be glad, for this your brother was dead and is alive; he was lost and is found" (Lk. 15:32). In the same chapter fifteen of St. Luke's Gospel, we read the parable of the sheep that was found (Lk. 15:3-6) and then the parable of the coin that was found. (Lk. 15:8ff.). Each time there is an emphasis on the same joy that is present in the case of the Prodigal Son. The father's fidelity to himself is totally concentrated upon the humanity of the lost son, upon

his dignity. This explains above all his joyous emotion at the moment of the son's return home.

The first deep reason for the emotional reception of the returned son is that the son's humanity has been saved, even if he has squandered his inheritance. Because "his humanity is saved" it can be "found again." What does this mean that "his humanity is saved" which according to the text is what the father's words to his elder son mean? Does this not contradict the previous statement concerning the loss of the "dignity of being a son" and the "awareness of squandered sonship"?

One needs to read the text twice. "The father's fidelity to himself is totally concentrated upon the humanity of the lost son, upon his dignity." There does not seem anything wrong with that but it implies something new and surprising, the "humanity" and the "dignity of being a son" are "saved"—despite his scandalous behaviour! And it is precisely that which is the source of the father's "joyous emotion at the moment of the son's return home."

The father's joy concerning the dignity of a son which has been saved is meant to be expressed in a similar way by the parables of the lost sheep and the lost coin.

Is this really what Jesus is announcing in his most beautiful parables?

6.3 The son never ceases to be the son of his father

The Pope goes further to find the reasons for the father's joy "at the moment of the son's return home." (*DiM* 6.3):

> Going on, one can therefore say that the love for the son, the love that springs from the very essence of fatherhood, in a way obliges the father to be concerned about his son's dignity. This concern is the measure of his love, the love of which Saint Paul was to write, "Love is patient and kind...love does not insist on its own way; it is not irritable or resentful...but rejoices in the right...hopes all things, endures all things" and "love never ends" (I Cor. 13:4-8). Mercy—as Christ has pre-

> sented it in the parable of the Prodigal Son—has the interior form of the love that in the New Testament is called *agape*. This love is able to reach down to every form of moral misery, to sin. When this happens, the person who is the object of mercy does not feel humiliated, but rather found again and "restored to value." The father first and foremost expresses to him his joy that he has been "found again" and that he has "returned to life." This joy indicates a good that has remained intact: even if he is a prodigal, a son does not cease to be truly his father's son; it also indicates a good that has been found again, which in the case of the Prodigal Son was his return to the truth about himself.

The decisive sentence is, "a son does not cease to be truly his father's son." This sentence says very clearly what has already been hinted at in many ways earlier (cf. *DiM* 5.6 & 6.3): the bond between father and son cannot be dissolved! Father remains father and son remains son.

Which makes the Pope's teaching as follows: the deepest reason for the indestructibility of the dignity of the son is the fatherhood of the father, the faithfulness of the father to himself. The faithfulness to his fatherhood is the guarantee for the mercy of God as father. This is called *agape* in the New Testament. It kept the humanity and the dignity of a son intact despite the scandalous behaviour of the Prodigal Son.

The return of the Prodigal Son "to the truth about himself" means quite simply the recognition of his nature given and, therefore, inviolable quality of being a son which comes to him when his father receives him with great joy.

6.4 Man's dignity: common experience of father and son

The Pope goes further into the relationship of the father and the son and reveals what he finds there (*DiM* 6.5):

> What took place in the relationship between the father and the son in Christ's parable is not to be evaluated "from the outside." Our prejudices about mercy are mostly the re-

> sult of appraising them only from the outside. At times it happens that by following this method of evaluation we see in mercy above all a relationship of inequality between the one offering it and the one receiving it. And, in consequence, we are quick to deduce that mercy belittles the receiver, that it offends the dignity of man. The parable of the Prodigal Son shows that the reality is different: the relationship of mercy is based on the common experience of that good which is man, on the common experience of the dignity that is proper to him. This common experience makes the Prodigal Son begin to see himself and his actions in their full truth (this vision in truth is a genuine form of humility); on the other hand, for this very reason he becomes a particular good for his father: the father sees so clearly the good which has been achieved thanks to a mysterious radiation of truth and love, that he seems to forget all the evil which the son had committed.

The idea "that mercy belittles the receiver, that it offends the dignity of man" has been expressed many times before. Now we learn that this is the wrong way of looking at it because it sees in mercy a relationship of (offensive) inequality. True mercy rests—*per consequentiam*—on a relationship of equality. The relationship of equality is at the same time the basis on which mercy as the "common experience of that good which is man" rests and is at all possible as the "the common experience of the dignity that is proper to him." The Pope is convinced that the parable of the Prodigal Son proves his thesis.

Later on in the Encyclical the Pope goes back to this theme (*DiM* 14.11):

> In analysing the parable of the Prodigal Son, we have already called attention to the fact that he who forgives and he who is forgiven encounter one another at an essential point, namely the dignity or essential value of the person, a point which cannot be lost and the affirmation of which, or its rediscovery, is a source of the greatest joy (cf. Lk. 15:32).

We may summarise the Pope's thoughts thus: In the parable of the Prodigal Son the blood bond between the father and the son is the foundation of an equality upon which their "common experience" of mercy rests and is possible. The object of this common experience is the inviolable value of the dignity of being man and a son.

We can now say quite concretely what the common experience is where the father and son meet:

From the father's side it is the son's being a son which is indeed a product of his fatherhood. The father has begotten the son and communicated to him for ever the basic value of the dignity of being a son.

From the son's side it is his humanity and his dignity of sonship which he possesses as a basic value because of his sonship from his father. This son's dignity is inviolable because it belongs to his nature and the father remains in constant faithfulness to his love and fatherhood.

In this way the "father and son meet" in a "common experience" of the inviolable good of the son's dignity of man.

This common experience becomes an event when the son returns home. It is described as an inner process as follows (*DiM* 6.4):

> The relationship of mercy is based on the common experience of that good which is man, on the common experience of the dignity that is proper to him. This common experience makes the Prodigal Son begin to see himself (= his inviolable son's dignity) and his actions in their full truth (this vision in truth is a genuine form of humility); on the other hand, for this very reason he becomes a particular good for his father: the father sees so clearly the good which has been achieved thanks to a mysterious radiation of truth and love, that he seems to forget all the evil which the son had committed.

The inner process which the Pope calls here a "common experience of mercy" of the father and the son is the conversion (*conversio*) though he does not use that word. It occurs, however, later in the following paragraph (*DiM* 6.5).

The aim of the Pope's exegesis of St. Luke's parable is to "understand exactly what the mercy of God consists in" (cf. *DiM* 6.1). That has been done. There now follows the review.

6.5 Conversion: the basic content of Christ's messianic message

After describing in detail the inner process of conversion (*DiM* 6.4) the Pope uses the word itself (*DiM* 6.5):

> The parable of the Prodigal Son expresses in a simple but profound way the reality of conversion. Conversion is the most concrete expression of the working of love and of the presence of mercy in the human world. The true and proper meaning of mercy does not consist only in looking, however penetratingly and compassionately, at moral, physical or material evil: mercy is manifested in its true and proper aspect when it restores to value, promotes and draws good from all the forms of evil existing in the world and in man. Understood in this way, mercy constitutes the fundamental content of the messianic message of Christ and the constitutive power of His mission. His disciples and followers understood and practised mercy in the same way. Mercy never ceased to reveal itself, in their hearts and in their actions, as an especially creative proof of the love which does not allow itself to be "conquered by evil," but overcomes "evil with good" (cf. Rom. 12:21). The genuine face of mercy has to be ever revealed anew. In spite of many prejudices, mercy seems particularly necessary for our times.

The "reality of conversion" is according to this "the most concrete expression of the working of love and of the presence of mercy in the human world." True mercy shows itself "when it restores to value, promotes and draws good from all the forms of evil existing in the world and in man." This is presented in the example of the conversion of the prodigal in the following way: In the "mysterious radiation" of the father's love the Prodigal Son recognises his inviolable dignity of being a son. The father's joy is so great over this that he "seems to forget all the evil which the son had committed" (*DiM* 6.4).

Unquestionably God's mercy constitutes "the fundamental content of the messianic message of Christ and the constitutive power of His mission." But there remains the question whether this "fundamental content" which the Pope has drawn out of the "common experience" of the father and the Prodigal Son is really the message of Jesus' parable.

6.6 The parable of the Prodigal Son in the Pope's allegory

In the Pope's exegesis we have an allegorical treatment of Jesus' parable of the Prodigal Son.

Interpreting isolated aspects of Jesus' parables in an allegorical way was already done in the early Church, mainly from St. Matthew, rarely from St. Luke. The reasons for an allegorical interpretation are due to the situation of the early Church which was in an hellenistic milieu, to the requirements of the mission but soon also to the desire to get to the deeper meaning of Jesus' parables.[3] The Encyclical similarly wants to help to a greater understanding of the deeper meaning of the parable of the Prodigal Son by an allegorical interpretation.

There is no difficulty in summarising the Encyclical's comments on Jesus' parable as an independent allegory of the Pope.[4] The papal allegory of the parable of the Prodigal Son is as follows:

The Prodigal Son is an analogy of the man of every period, beginning with Adam who first lost the inheritance of grace and original justice. The father in the parable is an analogy of God the Father.

---

3 Cf. Joachim Jeremias, [*The Parables of Jesus*] (Zurich 1952), pp. 50-70.

4 *Ibid.* allegorisation in the early Church (*e.g.*, Mt. 13:1-9 = Jesus' parable; Mt. 13:18-23 = the evangelist's allegory).

This son demanded his inheritance from his father. He received it, squandered it and ended up with the pigs. Then he thought about it and said to himself, "the hired labourers in my father's house have everything they need and here I die in wretchedness. I will go back to my father and serve him from now on as a hired labourer. That will certainly be a humiliation for me but I have lost my dignity of a son and according to the norms of justice I now only have the right to be a labourer in my father's house."

Thinking this he made the decision to go home. There he got a big surprise.

His father received the one who had grievously offended him by his scandalous behaviour, with exceeding great joy and lavished presents upon him. For the father saw the situation completely differently to the Prodigal Son: because of his constant faithfulness to himself, to his fatherhood, he knew that his son, even when he was far away never lost his dignity of being a son and never could. Even if his son hadn't seen that in his misery the basic value of his son's dignity remained intact. For the bond between father and son could never be dissolved!

The father's joy at the return of the Prodigal Son makes the son aware of this fact: even when he had previously thought that he had lost his dignity of being a son he now recognises the full truth about himself, his inviolable and therefore never lost dignity of being a son.

The double statement, that the son believed he had lost his dignity when he was far from home but now realised that he had never lost it is thus not *per se* a contradiction, but simply the transition of the consciousness of the son in misery to the consciousness of the son when he comes home. A change of consciousness which represents a "conversion" when he meets his overjoyed father.

The father's mercy is not a humiliation of the son. For mercy does not rest on a principle of inequality but equality. The inviolable bond between father and son is the foundation of their common experience of the basic value of the Prodigal Son's inviolable dignity of being a son. The recognition of this profound truth about himself which he receives when he is so joyfully accepted by his father is on the son's side the conversion process. On the father's side this process of his son's "finding himself" leads to the Prodigal Son being particularly dear to him. Then the father sees "so clearly the good which has been achieved thanks to a mysterious radiation of truth and love, that he seems to forget all the evil which the son had committed." Conversion and mercy are therefore necessary to one another. Mercy can be seen most clearly and truly when it restores to value, promotes and draws good from all the forms of evil existing in the world and in man. This is the "fundamental content of Christ's messianic message and the constitutive power of His mission."

6.7 Critical examination of the allegorical interpretation of the parable

In St. Luke's Gospel the parable of the Prodigal Son is a story out of real life,[5] in the Encyclical it becomes an allegory.

Considering that allegorical interpretations of Jesus' parables already exist in the Gospels themselves and continued under the heading of the many senses of Sacred Scripture,[6] it is quite legitimate for the Pope to try to explain one of Jesus' most beautiful parables in an allegorical interpretation for the people of his period, especially when this is done as a "development of the full power of the biblical message."[7]

The important points in the Pope's interpretation are the

---

5 *Ibid.* cf. p. 106.

6 Cf. Augustin Bea, in *Lexicon für Theologie und Kirche* (= *LThK*) (Freiburg i. Br. 1986), II, pp. 435ff.

7 Thus Karl Lehmann in his Herder commentary on *Dives in Misericordia*: [*Threatened Man and the Power of Mercy*] (Freiburg i. Br. 1981), p. 93.—Concerning the Encyclical's language and argumentation see *ibid.* pp. 96ff.

analogies (cf. *DiM* 5.2).

– The first analogy is: the Prodigal Son is the man of every period. But this is in contradiction to the parable as presented by St. Luke: the elder son is also a "man"! He behaved completely different to the "man for every period" to whom he also should belong. He did not forsake his father and did not squander his inheritance but rather served his father faithfully. The "elder brother" is—consistently enough—only fleetingly mentioned twice in the Pope's exegesis (cf. *DiM* 6.1 & 2). It is not without importance for the exegesis of the parable for it is a "twin peaked" parable and the elder son is the second peak and one that is especially stressed.[8]

The analogy does not just say the Prodigal Son is the man of every period but also the "man of every period, beginning with the one who was the first to lose the inheritance of grace and original justice" (*qui primus gratiae perdidit hereditatem pristinaeque honestatis*). This is a very significant thing to say dogmatically for Adam is also brought into this analogy and the *status iustitiae originalis* is his "inheritance."

At first sight the Encyclical seems to give the traditional teaching regarding the loss of original justice and to abandon the thesis of universal salvation.

On closer inspection, however, the way the Encyclical expresses itself is strange. For according to Church teaching it is not the "man of every period" who lost the state of grace but only our first parents. It was only our first parents who had this original grace therefore it was only they who could lose it.

The justice in their original state was also not an "inheritance" that was due to the first parents but rather a gift of grace. From whom could Adam have inherited, required or demanded this original state of grace and with which contemporaries could the first man have squandered this inheritance in a foreign land?

It is true that the first parents' original justice was to be at

[8] Joachim Jeremias, *op. cit.*, p. 108.

the same time an inherited justice for their descendants. But this intended inheritance was never inherited. The first parents lost "the original state of grace" and their descendants could neither inherit it, nor lose it nor pass it on. Adam's descendants began life with Original Sin *in statu naturae lapsae*.

The Encyclical's formulation is, however, not a slip of the pen. Rather the Pope by the sentence, "man of every period, beginning with the one who was the first to lose the inheritance of grace and original justice" is taking the analogy of his exegesis back to the "beginning" to the "mystery of the Creation and election" (cf. *DiM* 4.12). Thus he has fixed the paradigm of the New Testament—as he already did with the Old Testament (cf. above *DiM* 4.4)—firmly in his theology of the covenant. It is from this point of view that we are to understand the exegesis of the parable in the Encyclical. From this point of view the Prodigal Son is in fact like Adam "the man of every period." For in Adam God made an inviolable covenant with the whole of humanity *actu uno* with the Creation. This was broken by Adam but at the same time healed *a priori* by the Cross of Christ in Adam so that Cardinal Wojtyla could say, "All men from the beginning to the end of the world have been redeemed and justified by Christ through His Cross."[9]

From the point of view of his theology of the covenant and quoting Scripture the Pope can thus speak of "the man of every period" and the loss of "original justice" and at the same time announce the Redemption and justification of all men.

– the second analogy is: The father in the parable is "God the Father" (cf. *DiM* 6.1). This does not tie up with the sense of St. Luke's parable either for if we look at the words of the Prodigal Son himself he says, "Father, I have sinned against Heaven (=God) and thee" (Lk. 15:18 & 21). This shows clearly that the father in the parable is not God but an earthly fa-

[9] Karol Wojtyla, *Sign of Contradiction*, p. 101. For the indestructibility of God's image in man see *Redemptor Hominis* 13.3 and Part II/1, pp. 181-187.

ther.[10]

The difference does not seem to bc important since Jesus Himself uses the example of the earthly father in the parable against the critics of the Gospel: that is what your heavenly Father is like, so full of love and mercy![11] The earthly father is thus here not an analogy for the heavenly Father.

The difference is, however, of extreme importance in the Pope's exegesis because there the analogy of God as Father is extended to the relationship with the son. That means:

If—as the Encyclical says—the father in the parable is "God the Father," then the Prodigal Son in the parable is the natural son of the divine Father.

That is precisely the third analogy in the Encyclical: the natural, biological relationship of the earthly father with his Prodigal Son in the parable is an analogy of the relationship between God the Father and the man of every period.

All through Jesus' preaching runs the theme of the relationship between God and man. Jesus builds on the faith of His listeners. They knew God as a Father (cf. Deut. 32:6; II Ki. 7:14; *etc.*). It is this Father which he presents to them in such an insistent way. The prayer of his disciples is the "Our Father, who art in Heaven." He emphasises to them that they are children of their heavenly Father and must behave as such. And it is this relationship which is in question in the parable of the Prodigal Son. But it remains clear in Jesus' parable that the natural biological relationship of the earthly father to his son is not a physical fatherhood of God for all men. This is the case only for the only begotten Son, begotten from all eternity. The blood bond of the father and the Prodigal Son in Jesus' parable is simply not an analogy for a natural bond between the heavenly Father and man.

But that is the Pope's interpretation and forms in fact the

---

[10] Joachim Jeremias, *op. cit.* p. 106.

[11] *Ibid.* p. 108.

dogmatic basis of his interpretation: If the father in the parable is simply "God the Father" then the Prodigal Son and thus the natural relationship between the father and son must consistently be brought into the analogy. The most significant consequences of this analogy in the Encyclical are:

Just as the blood bond between the earthly father and the Prodigal Son is of its nature indissoluble so is the bond between the heavenly Father and the "man of every period." Just as the Prodigal Son as the natural son of his father cannot lose the dignity of his being a son and always remains the son of his father whatever he does, so man as son of the heavenly Father can never lose the basic value of his filial dignity, his being a son.

Of course the Pope knows that the natural relationship between a father and his son is in classical theology the preferred analogy to express the unique relationship between God the Father and His only begotten Son and therefore the metaphysical way in which Jesus Christ is the Son of God.[12] This unique relationship is extended in the Encyclical to the relationship between God as Father and the "man of every period" that is to the whole of humanity. The difference is that Christ is sinless whereas sinful but universally redeemed man must become aware of the full truth of his humanity, the inviolable dignity of his sonship.

This remarkable conclusion is just the consequence of the Pope's theology of the covenant and his concept of revelation: According to this the deepest humanity of each man which *a priori* he possesses as an inviolable basic value is his dignity of being a son because of his nature. The extension of the unique relationship between God the Father and the only begotten Son to man generally means that the way in which Christ is the Son is identical with the way in which the "man of every period" is the son. This means that Christ, the Son of God,

[12] Cf. Ludwig Ott, *Fundamentals of Catholic Dogma*, pp. 62ff.; 128ff.

who formally united Himself to every man by His Incarnation is humanity's universal principle of being. Christ Himself seen in this way is only the most perfect expression of that which every man, the whole of humanity, is ontologically.[13]

Thus we are once again faced with the alternative, as we were in the Pope's thesis of revelation's anthropocentrism and theocentrism:[14] "Either Christ is only man or man is divine."[15]

Doubtless the relationship of the earthly father to the Prodigal Son in Jesus' parable is also an analogy for the relationship of God to man. But man remains a wretched man compared to God as the parable describes him. If we look dogmatically at the concrete example in the biblical parable of the relationship of God to man then we may say from the point of view of classical theology:

God, the almighty Father, is the Creator of man. Man was not begotten but created in the image and likeness of God. The relationship of God to man consists of a double bond of nature and grace. The different qualities of this bond show themselves after the Fall of our first parents in a double consequence: The *imago Dei*, the natural image of God is wounded, the *similitudo Dei*, the supernatural likeness of God or sanctifying grace is lost.[16] Similarly every man who has been redeemed by the Cross of Christ and justified by faith loses this likeness of God through any mortal sin and breaks the bond of grace which joined him to God.[17] The likeness of God means a supernatural "likeness" of man with God. It is a *gratia creata* and not a consubstantial equality with God, not a *gratia increata*.

The double relationship of God to man is thus in no way

---

[13] The similarity to Henri de Lubac and Karl Rahner is remarkable. For the Pope's theology of the covenant see Part II/1, pp. 24-32 & pp. 118ff.

[14] See above *DiM* 1.4.

[15] *Ibid.* and Part I, p. 114.

[16] Cf. Ludwig Ott, *op. cit.* pp. 105ff.; 128ff.

[17] Denzinger-Schönmetzer, *Enchiridion Symbolorum* [Eng. ver. *The Sources of Catholic Dogma*] [= D], 808; 837; 862; 894; 899; 1290.

simply indissoluble and man's supernatural dignity of being a son is in no way impossible to lose as the Encyclical presents it. It simply ignores the necessary distinction of nature and grace in the relationship of God to man. In contrast to the classical teaching the Encyclical affirms the bond of God to man to be inviolable: both as the *imago Dei* and the *similitudo Dei*, both nature and grace. The third analogy similarly understands grace as being *increata*. The Encyclical goes into more details in Chapter V.

The fourth analogy in the Pope's exegesis is "man's interior" (cf. *DiM* 5.4). It manifests itself in the Prodigal Son's words which in his misery he says to himself and then, when he arrives home, to his father.

Exegetes are united in saying that these words of the Prodigal Son in a unique way express what contrition, penance, return and conversion mean for Jesus and the New Testament. Contrition and penance mean the decisive turning away from sin and the trusting and obedient turning back to God with nothing held back and no claim to rights. That is what St. Luke's parable of the Prodigal Son says about the "main problem" of conversion![18]

The Encyclical teaches something completely different. The Pope makes Jesus think things which are completely alien to Him. The most important biblical words contrition, penance and return are not mentioned, "conversion" is given another meaning.

In Jesus' parable the decision to return home matures in the Prodigal Son immediately out of the humiliations which he suffers in the foreign land and which he is no longer able to put up with. Such a degradation means he has no thoughts of the "humiliation and shame" which are to be associated with his return to his father's house. From the prodigal's words, "I no longer deserve to be called thy son; treat me as one of thy

---

[18] Karl Heinrich Rengstorf, [*The Gospel According to St. Luke*] (Göttingen 1967), NTD III, p. 185.

hired labourers" (Lk. 15:19), there is no sign of a consciousness of "the norms of justice" a claim to the right to work as a hired labourer in his father's house. The words are rather a completely humble plea without any sign of a right! The Prodigal Son has lost any "rights" by his behaviour. Such a claim, which is neither contained nor to be found in the son's words, would completely invalidate the act of contrition, penance, return and conversion in the sense that Jesus or the New Testament see them.

But that is precisely what happens in the Encyclical! From the conversion of the Prodigal Son which in Jesus' parable is an act of contrite decisiveness, a decisive turning away from his sinful life and a trusting, pleading turning to his father, we get in the Encyclical a pure process of consciousness. This is described in the following way: When his father receives him with great joy the Prodigal Son begins "to see himself and what he has done in the fullness of truth." And this happens according to the principle of equality and the "common experience" of father and son. The son recognises the inviolable basic value of his dignity as a son and sees in the light of this self-experience his earlier wrong behaviour.—What is described here is "conversion" based on equality. The relationship of father and son consists in a "familial" equality and mercy in a "common experience" of God as Father and man.

The full extent of the change of meaning which Jesus' parable undergoes with the magisterial authority of an Encyclical becomes clear when we confront the Pope's exegesis with a scientific exegesis. We will now present a general characterisation of the parable by Joachim Jeremias:

> The parable of the Prodigal Son is not an allegory but a story from real life as we see in the way God is named in vv. 18 & 21...
>
> The parable belongs to that group of parables that contain the essential Gospel which says, the time of salvation has come, the Saviour is here! Salvation has been sent—to the poor! Jesus has come—a Saviour for *sinners*!...

The parable is given for the opponents of this Gospel of salvation. It is a defence, a justification of the Gospel, a weapon in the fight against critics and enemies of the Gospel. The parable of the Prodigal Son should really be called the parable of the Father's love...

It portrays in an overwhelming simplicity the following: This is what God is like, so kind, so good, so full of mercy, so overflowing with love. He is overjoyed by the return of the lost as is the father who holds the feast. But this is only the first half (vv. 11-24); the parable has, however, two peaks: it shows not only the return of the younger son but also the protest of the elder. Since the first half is complete in itself it seems superfluous at first sight to add a second half. Why does Jesus add it on? There is only one answer: because of the concrete situation! The parable is for people who are like this elder brother, *i.e.,* for people who are scandalised by the Gospel. They should have their conscience pricked. Jesus says to *them*, that is how great God's love is for his lost children and you are miserable, harsh, ungrateful and self righteous! Be merciful! Do not be so harsh! The spiritually dead rise up, the lost find their home, rejoice! That is, just as in the other twin peaked parables, the emphasis is on the second peak. The parable of the Prodigal Son is therefore not so much an announcement of the Gospel to the poor as the justification of the Gospel for its critics. Jesus' own justification is due to God's love being so great. (Jesus claims God Himself to support his Gospel!) Jesus does not rest with a simple analogy. The parable is suddenly interrupted and the end remains open. This is meant to reflect the reality that confronts Jesus at that time. Jesus' listeners are in the elder son's situation and must decide whether they are going to follow the difficult words of the Father and rejoice. Jesus does not break the stick over their backs, He still has hope that they will overcome this stumbling block to the Gospel. The justification of the Gospel becomes a reproach and an attempt to win the hearts of His critics.[19]

[19] Joachim Jeremias, *op. cit.* pp. 106; 102ff.; 108ff.

The results of our analysis are: by importing analogies that are foreign to the text of the biblical parable the Pope has brought in the principles of knowledge of his *nouvelle théologie* loaded with his own favourite special philosophical ideas. Thus he himself has laid the foundations for his own exegesis. On this foundation Jesus' parable becomes an allegory of the Pope's theology. At the same time, the biblical parable,which is a paradigm for the New Testament, is simply the supplier of material for the presentation of his own theology. The "fundamental content of Christ's messianic message" undergoes in this way a radical and profound change.

CHAPTER V

Completion of the Messianic Mission in the Paschal Mystery*

The fifth Chapter continues the exegesis of the New Testament and reaches the Encyclical's theological high point: the completion of the messianic mission in the Paschal mystery. The Pope first presents the revelation of mercy in the Passion and Resurrection (7) then he confronts the Paschal mystery with evil in the history of man (8). With the "mother of mercy" (9) the main theological section of the Encyclical which is full of references to Sacred Scripture comes to a close (Ch. II-V).[1]

7. The revelation of mercy in the Passion and Resurrection**

The seventh article is the first main section of John Paul II's teaching on the Redemption in *Dives in Misericordia.*

7.1 The human and divine dimension of the Redemption

The Pope takes up where he left off in the last article (6) and continues (*DiM* 7.1):

> The messianic message of Christ and His activity among people end with the cross and resurrection.[2] We have to pen-

---

* Chapter title in the English translation, "The Paschal Mystery."

** Chapter title in the English translation, "Mercy Revealed in the Cross and Resurrection."

[1] Cf. INTRODUCTION, 2. Outline and Arrangement (p. 18).

[2] The Ascension is missing from the English translation.

> etrate deeply into this final event—which especially in the language of the Council is defined as the *Mysterium Paschale*—if we wish to express in depth the truth about mercy, as it has been revealed in depth in the history of our salvation. At this point of our considerations, we shall have to draw closer still to the teaching (*Magisterium*) of the Encyclical *Redemptor Hominis.* If, in fact, the reality (*veritas*) of the Redemption, in its human dimension, reveals the unheard-of greatness of man, *qui talem ac tantum meruit habere Redemptorem*, (cf. Holy Saturday liturgy "*Exultet*") at the same time the divine dimension of the Redemption enables us, I would say, in the most empirical and "historical" way, to uncover the depth of that love which does not recoil (*abhorret*) before the extraordinary sacrifice of the Son, in order to satisfy the fidelity of the Creator and Father towards human beings, created in His image and chosen from "the beginning," in this Son, for grace and glory (*ut satis faciat Creatoris ac Patris fidelitati erga homines eius ad imaginem effectos iamque a "principio" electos in gratiam et gloriam*).

The Pope begins his teaching on the Redemption with a reference to his principle of knowledge. He repeats what he has already said in a general way in the introduction to the whole Encyclical: *Redemptor Hominis* is the presupposition for *Dives in Misericordia.* The principle of "double revelation" is also valid for considering the Paschal mystery which means:

– the "human dimension of the truth of the Redemption" or the *a priori* revelation is the same as the axiom of universal salvation. That is why, as the quoted text says, the content of this revelation is not the "*felix culpa*" from Holy Saturday's *Exultet* but in an extraordinary changing of meaning "the unheard-of greatness of man who deserved to have such and so great a redeemer."

– "the divine dimension of the truth of the Redemption" or the *a posteriori* revelation is identical to the historical revelation. It is related to the *a priori* revelation and reveals to man his "unheard-of greatness" by, in and through Christ, "revealing in the most empirical and "historical" way the depth of the Father's love." The Encyclical *Dives in Misericordia* is dedicated to this revelation (cf. *DiM* 1.1 & 1.2) and especially this fifth chapter with its emphasis on the teaching on the Redemption. Thus it is said from the beginning that humanity is *ab origine* in a state of effectively being redeemed and that the historical revelation of the Father in Christ is basically to reveal the depth of the Father's love which has *a priori* given man his unheard-of greatness.

The Pope does not just give the theological principles in advance but immediately draws from them the fundamental thesis of his teaching on Redemption. This is:

The depth of the Father's love for man shows itself by giving the Son "in order to satisfy the fidelity of the Creator and Father towards human beings, created in His image and chosen from "the beginning," in this Son, for grace and glory."

The thesis means the definitive predestination of the whole of humanity to grace and glory "*a principio.*" On this foundation follows logically the radical shift in meaning of the sacrifice of the cross: It is the satisfaction for the constant faithfulness of the Father to this very covenant with man *a principio.* In this sense the axiom of universal salvation or rather universal giving of grace is the centre of the Encyclical's teaching on Redemption. It is a teaching of the Redemption of people who are effectively redeemed and justified *a priori.* The traditional conception of Redemption is given a whole new meaning by the principle of universal giving of grace *a principio.*

7.2 The suffering Messiah receives no mercy from man

The Pope turns first to the suffering side of the Paschal mystery and begins his teaching on Redemption—like any theological treatise[3]—with the person of the Redeemer (*DiM* 7.2):

[3] The teaching on God the Redeemer is normally the forerunner of Christian anthropology with the teaching on Original Sin. In the Encyclical it is the thesis of the universal giving of grace (*DiM* 7.1).

> The events of Good Friday and, even before that, in prayer in Gethsemane, introduce a fundamental change into the whole course of the revelation of love and mercy in the messianic mission of Christ. The one who "went about doing good and healing" (Acts 10:38) and "curing every sickness and disease" (Mt. 9:35) now Himself seems to merit the greatest mercy and to appeal* for mercy, when He is arrested, abused, condemned, scourged, crowned with thorns, when He is nailed to the cross and dies amidst agonising torments (cf. Mk. 15:37; Jn. 19:30). It is then that He particularly deserves mercy from the people to whom He has done good, and He does not receive it. Even those who are closest to Him cannot protect Him and snatch Him from the hands of His oppressors.
>
> At this final stage of His messianic activity the words which the prophets, especially Isaiah, uttered concerning the Servant of Yahweh are fulfilled in Christ: "Through his stripes we are healed" (Is. 53:5).

According to the careful and restrained text the events in Gethsemane and on Good Friday show a "fundamental change" in the mission of the Messiah: Christ, who in His whole life has shown mercy to man becomes in His Passion an object of mercy for man. But His expectation of experiencing help and mercy, especially from them that are closest to Him, is disappointed.

This thesis goes right to the centre of the previous teaching of the Church on the Redemption. For:

A Messiah who expects help and deliverance from his suffering from man does not carry His cross willingly! Thence the fearful question:

Did Christ really hope for such mercy from man in His

* The Latin text says, "*nunc contra ipse plurimam promereri videtur misericordiam eamque evocare.*" The English translation is thus inaccurate. It is *evocare* not *invocare*. In general, however, the Encyclical has the basic idea.

Passion so that one can speak of a "fundamental change...in the messianic mission of Christ"?

The answer can be found in Sacred Scripture: In the Gospels it is stressed with every emphasis that Christ accepted his redeeming sufferings absolutely voluntarily. He had predicted his terrible sufferings. Knowing about these sufferings he went up to Jerusalem voluntarily. He neither appealed* for the mercy of man nor did He want or expect "to be freed from the hands of his enemies." Rather He decisively rejected any attempt to hold Him back from His Passion, to "protect Him and snatch Him from the hands of His oppressors" (cf. Mt. 16:22ff.; 22:49ff.). Indeed Christ's messianic mission consisted precisely in redeeming man by His absolutely voluntary sacrifice of atonement![4]

How Christ answered any such well-meaning attempt to hold him back from His journey to His Passion in Jerusalem is seen in the Gospel with Simon Peter at Caesarea Philippi. Christ rejected the worried attempts of the Apostle to restrain Him from accepting His sufferings and death with the words, "Get thee behind me, Satan! Thou art a scandal unto me: because thou savourest not the things that are of God, but the things that are of men" (Mt. 16:23). That is how the Lord Himself characterises the pious considerations of Peter's successor concerning the "truth of mercy" and the "fundamental change...in the messianic mission of Christ." Christ likewise rejects his disciple's attempts to free Him from the hands of his persecutors by the sword with the words, "Thinkest thou that I cannot ask my Father, and he will give me presently more than twelve legions of angels? How then shall the scriptures be fulfilled, that so it must be done?" (Mt. 26:53ff.).

We are forced by Holy Scripture to disagree with the Encyclical: Even in the Passion of Christ there is no appeal for the mercy of man, there is no expectation to be delivered from the hands of his enemies, there is therefore no "fundamental

---

[4] D. 86; 223; 314; 333; 570; 711; 718; 747; 794.

change...in the messianic mission of Christ." This thesis has no support in the Gospel.

The question remains: where does the Encyclical get this thesis from? The question can easily be answered. The Pope develops his idea from the relationship between equality and the common experience in mercy (*DiM* 6.4), by adding a third element: reciprocity.

The Pope himself gives a more precise definition of reciprocity in mercy later on in the Encyclical. There he says that mercy cannot work in only one direction. Rather, following the "example of Christ," the principle is (*DiM* 14.3):

> An act of merciful love is only really such when we are deeply convinced at the moment we perform it that we are at the same time receiving mercy from the people who are accepting it from us. If this bilateral and reciprocal quality is absent, our actions are not yet true acts of mercy, nor has there yet been fully completed in us that conversion to which Christ has shown us the way by His words and example, even to the cross, nor are we yet sharing fully in the magnificent source of merciful love that has been revealed to us by Him.

According to this Christ Himself gave the example that a true act of mercy must be reciprocal. That is why Christ also had to have the expectation in His Passion of receiving man's mercy and help for His mercy to be real.

The thesis of reciprocity in mercy is the third main idea in the Pope's teaching on Redemption.

By importing such ideas into the very centre of the redemptive work of Christ the Encyclical in a careful and pious way formulates the essence of the Redeemer and His Passion. A Redeemer who in His Passion appeals for or expects man's mercy but finds none, who hopes to be freed by His followers from the hands of his enemies but is disappointed is not, however, the Christ of the Gospels.

7.3 The suffering Messiah appeals in vain for mercy from the Father

Christ now turns in His suffering "as man" to the Father (*DiM* 7.3):

> Christ, as the man who suffers really and in a terrible way in the Garden of Olives and on Calvary, addresses Himself to the Father—that Father whose love He has preached to people, to whose mercy He has borne witness through all of His activity. But He is not spared—not even He—the terrible suffering of death on the cross: "For our sake God made him to be sin who knew no sin," (II Cor. 5:21), St. Paul writes, summing up in a few words the whole depth of the Cross and at the same time the divine dimension of the reality of the Redemption (*indolem divinam veritatis Redemptionis*).

The Pope draws a parallel with the preceding paragraph. This is carefully and impressively built up on the foundation of the reciprocity of mercy: Just as Christ in His Passion is said to have appealed for help in vain from man (*DiM* 7.2), so now he turns "as man" who suffers in a terrible way in His Passion to the Father—also in vain.

From this presentation follows in cold logic what the author probably does not see:

A father who answers the call for mercy of his son in terrible sufferings to spare him these sufferings by "making him to be sin who knew no sin" and handing him over to these terrible sufferings, acts in a capricious and merciless way. The punishment of the innocent instead of the guilty makes no sense since a punishment *per se* can only be given to a person who has deserved it. Otherwise it would completely lose its point, indeed completely take away the moral meaning of sin and the moral order itself.[5] That is precisely what happens in

[5] Matthias Joseph Scheeben, *Handbuch der katholischen Dogmatik* [*Handbook of Catholic Dogma*] [= *Dogmatik*] (Freiburg i. Br. 1954), Collected writings V/2, no. 1304.

the text of the Encyclical and is not cancelled by the later revelation of the Father's love in raising his Son from the dead (cf. *DiM* 7.4; 8.6).

Using biblical language the Encyclical covers up the terrible contents of what is said.

The formulation that Christ "as man" turned to the Father must not make us forget that Christ always acts as God and man. That alone gives the divine dimension to the work of Redemption and stops Christ's acts from being something purely human. Only because Christ is God and man can he wipe out sin by His work of Redemption and reconcile us with God.

According to how the Pope sees it, Christ's appeal to His Father, whose mercy He has preached, presupposes the expectation of receiving mercy from the Father: "If this reciprocity is missing, then our actions are not yet true acts of mercy" (cf. *DiM* 7.2; 14.3). Christ's appeal to the Father for mercy is then to be understood in the sense of a real request and a firm hope that he will be spared the suffering. But that would be "a fundamental change in Christ's messianic mission." For the Son of God became man to redeem us by His Passion. Does the Gospel really show a desperate plea from the Son for mercy and through this a break in the centre of Christ's messianic mission?

Jesus Himself gives the definitive answer to this question before His sufferings, "Now is my soul troubled. And what shall I say? Father, save me from this hour. But for this cause I came unto this hour. Father, glorify thy name" (Jn. 12:27ff.). Thus He directly refuses to ask the Father to keep Him from the Passion. In sovereign willingness He fulfils His messianic mission as Redeemer of the world to the glory of the Father.

The Encyclical gives no authority for its thesis. The only thing mentioned is Christ's prayer in the Garden of Olives, "My Father, if it be possible, let this chalice pass from me. Nevertheless not as I will, but as thou wilt" (Mt. 26:39). Can this moving text be used to back the Pope's thesis?

The prayer reveals Christ's agony but at the same time His overcoming it by giving Himself up to the will of the Father. It shows the Messiah in His last great temptation which he overcomes victoriously (cf. Mt. 26:36-46).[6] Jesus' prayer is not a vain appeal for the Father to spare Him the Passion but the Son of man's great *Fiat* in His agony to God's plan of Redemption.[7] In St. Luke an angel appears from Heaven, not to take the chalice away but to give Him strength to bring the sacrifice to completion (Lk. 22:43), to which He has dedicated Himself (Jn. 17:1ff.).[8] And Jesus accepts the chalice.

If we accept the Pope's thesis then the prayer would have to be—without any *Fiat*—"Father, have mercy on me! Spare me this hour and spare me this terrible suffering!"

Because there is no vain plea of the Son for the Father's mercy to spare Him the Passion, thus II Cor. 5:21 is not the answer of an unmerciful and capricious God. Just as in the case of Christ's appeal for mercy from man so also in this appeal for mercy from the Father the same decisive inner significance of Christ's mission is ignored—the Son's absolute free choice, His *Fiat* which He had spoken even as He came into the world (Heb. 10:5ff.) and confirmed before His suffering in Gethsemane. Christ's Passion as a sacrifice for sin as St. Paul expresses it in II Cor. 5:21 is wholly determined by the Son's *Fiat*. Through his voluntary acceptance of humanity's guilt of sin Christ Himself becomes in no way a sinner.

Considered from the side of sinful man the satisfaction rendered by the third party involves the transfer of the evil of punishment from the sinner to an innocent but this is by no means the punishment of an innocent instead of the guilty. Rather the taking away of the guilt is essentially conditioned by the free, loving acceptance of the suffering of the punish-

---

[6] Cf. Julius Schniewind, *Das Evangelium nach Matthäus* [*The Gospel According to Matthew*] (Göttingen 1964), NTD II pp. 259ff.—Karl Staab, *Das Evangelium nach Matthäus* (Würzburg 1951), Echter-Bibel, p. 145.

[7] *Ibid.*

[8] *Ibid.*

ment and the great favour that he enjoys with God.[9]

There is another inner significance which cannot be overlooked and which is added to the Son's *Fiat* according to the Church's oral and written tradition. This significance is the high majesty of the Redeemer that not only influences the Messiah's whole way of acting but also makes the death on the cross a sacrifice of sovereign devotion. We see this significance in the Lord's words, "The Father loves me because I lay down my life, that I may take it again. No man taketh it away from me: but I lay it down of myself, and I have power to lay it down: and I have power to take it up again. This commandment I have received of my Father" (Jn. 10:17ff.).

Christ is not only the sacrificial lamb who speaks His *Fiat* out of obedience but also the sacrificial priest. As head of mankind and consubstantial Son of the Father He offers Himself in sovereign freedom and in divine authority over His own life as a victim for sin for the sins of men. The high priestly sacrifice of Christ leaves no room for a Messiah who in His Passion "as man" appeals to the Father for mercy to take away the suffering and who only passively suffers the Cross as a punishment for our sins.

The Pope's "biblical" grounds for his teaching on Redemption has in fact no support in the Bible. Rather the omission of the important inner significance in the Redeemer's actions leads to a further distortion of the biblical figure of Christ.

– Misinterpreting the Redeemer leads necessarily to misinterpreting His work of Redemption. The key text of this misinterpretation is for the Pope II Cor. 5:21. Obviously St. Paul's words uncover "the depth of the mystery of the Cross," but not in the way the Encyclical interprets them. That is, however, what is meant as we see when the Pope continues his train of thought and says (*DiM* 7.3):

> Indeed this (form of) Redemption (*Quae quidem ipsa*

---

[9] Matthias Joseph Scheeben, *op. cit.* no. 1304.

> *redemptio*) is the ultimate and definitive revelation (*definitiva patefactio*) of the holiness of God, who (*ipse*) is the absolute fullness of perfection: (The) fullness of justice and of love, since justice is based on love, flows from it and tends towards it. In the passion and death of Christ—in the fact that the Father did not spare His own Son, but "for our sake made him sin" (*ibid.*)—absolute justice is expressed, for Christ undergoes the passion and cross because of the sins of humanity. This constitutes even a "superabundance" of justice, for the sins of man are "compensated for" by the sacrifice of the Man-God.

According to this II Cor. 5:21 would be in the Pope's interpretation the definitive revelation of the Redemption of the holiness, love and justice of God.

The quoted text as it stands sounds absolutely good and Catholic (cf. D 799). But there is a fundamental shift of meaning: In II Cor. 5:21 St. Paul presupposes the truth of faith of Original Sin, the Encyclical the axiom of universal salvation.

This hardly noticeable change of meaning in the centre of the work of Redemption concerns the very centre of the Pope's teaching on the Redemption. That is why it must be explained in the context of the Encyclical.

The quoted text says only a part of the truth: Christ "suffered His Passion and Cross for the sins of men" But the most important thing is not said here—to whom this satisfaction is made—because this is already clear from what has been said, especially in the fundamental thesis of the Pope's teaching on the Redemption at the beginning of this article (cf. *DiM* 7.1). With reference to this thesis the complete sense of what the Encyclical says is as follows:

In the Son's sacrifice on the cross the Father has "in the most empirical and "historical" way," revealed the depth of His love for man. He gave His innocent and sinless Son for us made as sin and handed Him over to suffering and the cross so that this faithfulness of the Father and Creator to man made in His image and likeness and chosen for grace *a principio* should do satisfaction for the sins of humanity. This election means the thesis of universal Redemption or giving of grace.

The decisive point is thus: The Father gives His Son as satisfaction for the sins of humanity not to redeem them from Original Sin but because the Father, even considering the sins of humanity, is constant in his faithfulness to his covenant of grace *ab origine* with universally redeemed man (cf. also Part II/1, pp. 118ff.).

This would conform to the traditional teaching of the Church if it meant that the Father revealed His love for man by giving His only begotten Son (cf. Jn. 3:16), so that He could perform satisfaction to the Father by His sacrifice on the cross for the sins of men in their place, to release them from the "slavery of sin" and to reconcile them to God. When we talk about sin we mean primarily the general sin of mankind, Original Sin but also following on from that all other sins committed as a consequence.

In the Pope's teaching on Redemption this central mystery of Redemption is rather different: Since God as Creator and Father in absolute faithfulness to man honours the covenant of grace with man—despite his sins—man is in an inviolable state of grace and salvation. The sacrifice of the Son for the sins of man has therefore a completely different character. The Father delivers His Son up to the death on the cross as a satisfaction for His own faithfulness to the inviolable covenant of grace which He made with universally redeemed man (cf. *DiM* 6).

Therefore in the Encyclical the words of St. Paul in II Cor. 5:21 revealing God's absolute holiness and justice have a new meaning and content: *Because* the Father—despite the sins of man—remains united with humanity in inviolable faithfulness *ab origine* in a covenant of grace, His absolute holiness and justice requires satisfaction for the sins of man. That is why the Father makes the Son as a sin for us and delivers Him up to suffering and death.

It should, however, be clear that the idea of an inviolable

faithfulness of God to an indestructible holy covenant of grace with man, who commits the most terrible sins, insults God's holiness in a most flagrant way. The idea of an absolute faithfulness of the Father to the axiom of universal giving of grace eliminates the dogma of Original Sin and means in the end nothing but a senseless clinging of a holy God to a covenant with man which remains intact despite any sin. The idea of such a covenant is a utopia which utterly insults God's holiness.

Such a distortion of St. Paul's words in II Cor. 5:21 is also of course no revelation of the absolute holiness and justice of God.

Only in the authentic history of salvation in the New Testament is the Cross the revelation of the absolute holiness, justice and love of God, and the Redemption of man by the Passion of the Man-God the divine measure of justice and the "abundance" of divine mercy (cf. D 550),—and the cross for each who believes not foolishness nor a scandal but the strength of God and His wisdom (cf. I Cor. 1:22-24).

– After talking about the Person and actions of the Redeemer the Pope comes to the "Fruits of salvation." What sort of fruits these are we see in the following passage (*DiM* 7.3):

> Nevertheless, this justice, which is properly justice "to God's measure," springs completely from love: from the love of the Father and of the Son, and completely bears fruit in love. Precisely for this reason the divine justice revealed in the cross of Christ is "to God's measure," because it springs from love and is accomplished in love, producing fruits of salvation (*quia oritur ex amore in amoreque perficitur, dum fructus parit salutis*). The divine dimension of Redemption is put into effect not only by bringing justice to bear upon sin, but also by restoring to love that creative power in man thanks to which he once more has access to the fullness of life and holiness that come from God (*Ratio divina Redemptionis non solum completur, cum peccatum vindicatur, sed cum amori redditur illa vis in homine creatrix, ob quam is accedere iterum valet ad vitae plenitudinem ac sanctimoniam a Deo procedentem*). In

> this way, Redemption involves the revelation of mercy in its fullness (*plenitudine*).

It is a question then of the fruits of salvation from the tree of divine justice and love which the Cross reveals. The actual substance of this justice and love has already been analysed and described in the previous paragraph.

According to the text,the fruits of salvation of that justice and love belong, as we might have expected to "the divine dimension of the Redemption" that is to the dimension of empirical history of salvation. So it is already clear that these fruits which the Cross is said to reveal are not the fruits of Redemption in their traditional sense that is of the justification and salvation of man. For the Redemption and justification of all men from the beginning to the end of the world belong in the Pope's theology to the "human dimension of the Redemption," the dimension of the *a priori* universal giving of grace.

The text of the Encyclical distinguishes two sorts of fruits of salvation in the "divine dimension of salvation": the "bringing justice to bear upon sin" and the renewal of the "creative power in man." The judgment of sin which was performed by the offering of the Son is merely mentioned. It has just been dealt with in the Encyclical in some detail. Now it is the turn of the "creative power in man."

The original nature of this "fruit of salvation" which the Cross is said to reveal becomes clear when it is compared with the "fruits of Redemption" in the traditional teaching of the Church:

According to this, the prerequisite for the work of Redemption is the absolute need of humanity to be redeemed since from the time of Adam it is in a state of Original Sin.

In order to redeem man from this state of being far from God and to reconcile him with Him, Christ accepted the Passion and through His sacrifice on the cross earned all fruits of the Redemption for the whole human race. These fruits are according to Matthias Joseph Scheeben,

> negatively the freeing from evil especially the forgiveness of sin and the punishments due to them and the taking away of the slavery to the devil; positively the giving of supernatural grace which is necessary for man to obtain eternal salvation. Above all there is also sanctifying grace belongs to the fruit of reparation and, in it, the reconciliation with God or the possession of friendship with God, being His child and finally the "opening of Heaven's Gate."[10]

Theoretically the divine Redeemer could have applied His reparative merits unconditionally to every individual immediately. But according to the whole of written and oral tradition that is not the case. The fruits of salvation do not fall automatically into man's lap but they must be applied to each individual by Christ and likewise accepted by each individual being with reason and will. The application and acceptance of the fruits of Redemption happens in the process of justification and is linked with the fulfilment of certain subjective conditions—penance, faith, baptism. The Church teaches the objective but not the subjective universality of the Redemption. The clearly defined concept of "justification" (cf. D 792ff.) never occurs in the Encyclical.

According to the Encyclical's teaching man finds himself principally in a state of being redeemed and not in a state of Original Sin. This state of salvation belongs in the Pope's terminology to the "human dimension of the Redemption" and contains the inviolable giving of grace to the whole of humanity *ab origine*. That is why the individual man needs no special application of the fruits of Redemption. That is why in the "divine dimension of the Redemption" it is simply a question of the judgment over sin as satisfaction for the absolute faithfulness of the Father to His never broken covenant of grace

[10] *Ibid.*, no. 1326.—concerning the following paragraph cf. Ludwig Ott, *Fundamentals of Catholic Dogma*, pp. 252ff.

with man and "that creative power in man" which, once love has been returned, makes man capable or reaching the "fullness" of the divine life. But that is only a process of consciousness in a man who was always in possession of the inviolable dignity of being a son.

It is, nonetheless, the teaching of the Church that since Original Sin "that creative power" is absolutely no longer "in man." Classical theology has been through this point carefully. It does not speak of a "*vis in homine creatrix*" but of a "*potentia oboedientialis,*" a passive capacity in man to receive the fruits of the Redemption. "A natural positive disposition to grace cannot exist due to Original Sin, because there is no inner proportion between nature and grace."[11] The Church teaches the absolute need of Redemption for every man and for the whole of humanity (cf. Rom. 3:9ff.).

7.4 The revelation of mercy in its completeness

The central problem of the teaching on Redemption in the Encyclical is that God's covenant of grace with man *ab origine*, because of the Father's faithfulness to his fatherhood in spite of all man's sins, remains indissoluble and intact. The Pope solves this problem by going to the centre of his teaching step by step.

First of all he draws the conclusion from what he said in the previous paragraph (*DiM* 7.4):

> The Paschal Mystery is therefore (*ideo*) the culmination of this revealing and effecting of mercy, which is able to justify man, to restore justice (*potest iustum facere iustitiamque ipsam reficere*) in the sense of that salvific order which God willed from the beginning in man and, through man, in the world (*quem ab initio Deus in homine optaverat ac per hominem in mundo*).
>
> The suffering Christ speaks in a special way to man, and

[11] Ludwig Ott, *op. cit.*, pp. 117; 273.

> not only to the believer. The non-believer also will be able to discover in Him the eloquence of solidarity with the human lot, as also the harmonious fullness of a disinterested dedication to the cause of man, to truth and to love.

The review of what has just been said (*DiM* 7.3) appears this time in traditional language but which has a new meaning: The restoration of God's wounded justice consists according to this in the offering of the Son so that He can make satisfaction for the sins of man to the faithfulness of the Father due to his inviolable covenant of grace with man *ab origine*. The "making man just" is linked to "that creative power in man" and means that it makes man, who *a priori* possesses his inviolable dignity of being a son, capable of advancing to "the fullness" of the divine life (cf. *DiM* 7.3).

This form of the realisation of mercy is done, or added, in the sense of the salvific order "which God willed from the beginning in man and through man in the world."

In the salvific order of the New Testament it is by no means simply man "in whom and through whom" God brought about the Redemption of the world but alone in Christ "in whom and through whom" God wrought the Redemption. As Head of humanity Christ perfects the work of the Redemption by offering Himself to God in man's place as a propitiatory sacrifice and making reparation for our sins. Man is the "object" of the Redemption absolutely in need of being redeemed. He must *let himself* be redeemed from the hopeless state of Original Sin and be reconciled with God (cf. II Cor. 5:20). In the New Testament there is no self-Redemption. Christ's action of taking our place and being the means of the Redemption is a *ministerium* that He alone offers to God in the name of humanity and which He alone *can* offer. For it is a substantial part of the *ministerium* that Christ Himself is God and in the work of Redemption as the perfect intermediary between God and man acts in His own name due to His divine authority (Heb. 9:11ff.). Due to His own divine authority He Himself makes His service of reparation effectively valid, He ratifies it and guarantees the acceptance of the same by God.[12]

Of course the Pope knows this teaching of the Church. It sounds like an antithesis when he says, God perfects the work of Redemption according to the salvific order from the beginning "in and through man." This new thesis is only understandable under the presupposition that the universal divine principle of Redemption exists in man himself from the beginning. Once again we are confronted with the question: Is man—like Christ—God?

The Pope does not give an answer. He continues with the Paschal mystery which reveals the true nature of man and his ontological relationship to the Father (*DiM* 7.4):

> And yet the divine dimension of the Paschal Mystery goes still deeper. The cross on Calvary, the cross upon which Christ conducts His final dialogue with the Father, emerges from the very heart of the love that man, created in the image and likeness of God, has been given as a gift, according to God's eternal plan (*Crux...exsurgit quasi de illius amoris medullis, quo ipse homo ad imaginem Dei ac similitudinem conditus aequabiliter secundum aeternum Dei consilium est honestatus*).

According to this the "divine dimension of the Paschal mystery" reveals the Father's love for man and, by so doing, man's essence. This revelation consists of three theses:

– It is the Father's love out of which according to the eternal salvific order, man as God's image (*imago*) and likeness (*similitudo*) has been created, or given existence, as an equal.[13] Therefore the image and likeness of God constitute the essence of man and together make up his nature.

In classical theology the *imago Dei* means the natural image of God, *i.e.,* man as God's creature. The *similitudo Dei* means the *supernatural* likeness to God, *i.e.,* man as a child of God

---

[12] Matthias Joseph Scheeben, *op. cit.*, no. 1275.

[13] The root meaning of *condere*—to put together—should show what is meant.

by sanctifying grace. If the natural image and the supernatural likeness of God make up together man's nature then nature and supernature are the same thing. Because this unity makes up the essence of man it is also indissoluble. Overcoming the traditional distinction between nature and grace has been one of the main aims of the *nouvelle théologie* since Maurice Blondel.

According to traditional Church teaching Adam himself is created as the natural image and supernatural likeness of God. But these two do not make "*conditus aequabiliter*" man's nature. The supernatural likeness is sanctifying grace. It is not part of man's nature but is a pure gift from God: a created supernatural gift "*quoad substantiam*," *i.e.*, it is a *gratia creata* which in its inner substance goes beyond the being, strength and requirements of created nature. Because it is not part of man's nature is is also possible to lose it. It was lost by Adam's sin and is lost through every mortal sin.[14]

Man's sin and God's holiness are mutually exclusive. God loves the repentant sinner who does penance and gives him then once more His grace, but there is no indissoluble covenant of grace between God and man in mortal sin.

– The next statement in the text of the Encyclical is the Father's love for man and for His only begotten Son emerges from the very heart of that love. The love is therefore the same.

An identical love is, however, only possible if the object of love is identical in substance and nature. In the identical love of the Father for man *and* for His Son on the cross, the love for man is even the more important. From this we see the Pope's thesis which changes the original meaning but which keeps repeating that it is the greatness of man which deserved such a Redeemer (cf. "*Exultet*" of the Paschal Vigil) and for which the Father gave His only begotten Son.[15] How great this greatness of man must be!

– Finally we see in the Encyclical the Father's love for man

---

[14] Ludwig Ott, *op. cit.*, pp. 294ff.; 304.

[15] Particularly emphasised *RH* 10. Cf. Part II/1, pp. 131-141.

is specific. It is identical with the Father's love for His Son on the cross.

If it is the same love of the Father for His Son on the cross, out of which man emerges as an equal in the image and likeness of God, then man was created also as redeemer and justifier, then man bears *ab origine* the features of Christ's countenance, then Adam is the first "anonymous Christian."[16]

But the Encyclical does not stop there. The Pope himself gives an additional explanation of the link that unites God to man in such a close way (*DiM* 7.4):

> God, as Christ has revealed Him, does not merely remain closely linked with the world as the Creator and the ultimate source of existence. He is also Father: He is linked to man, whom He called to existence in the visible world, by a bond still more intimate than that of Creation. It is love which not only creates the good but also grants participation in the very life of God: Father, Son and Holy Ghost. For he who loves desires to give himself (*donare se ipsum*).

According to this God is and remains linked to each man by a double ontological bond:

– an intimate bond links God as creator and source of life with His Creation (*Deus...arctis cum mundo vinculis colligatur uti Creator primusque ipsius vitae fons*). This bond links God to man as the created, natural *imago Dei*. This relationship between Creator and creature is *cum grano salis* comparable with that of an artist and his work.

– a closer bond links God as Father with man whom He has called into existence and created as His natural image

[16] Concerning the idea that the original creative intent of God was not to send a non-suffering Christ, M.J. Scheeben writes (*op. cit.* no. 1384), "Rather we should think of Christ perfected in Himself and perfecting the world by His cross as what God intended originally in the Creation in the same way that Christ's sacrifice of the Cross was not intended in the Scotist sense as a remedy for sin but as the concrete form of the highest perfection of the world and revelation of God."

(*Pater...cum homine a se vocato ad vitam in mundo aspectabili ducendam coniungitur nexu aliquo vel strictiore quam Creationis*), by God giving Himself as a gift to man as Father and thereby making man His child. This bond rests on God's true fatherhood, comparable with the relationship of an earthly father with his natural son.

Since no further distinction follows, we are here dealing with a substantial union of God with man, the uniting of man as God's created image to the indissoluble unity of image and likeness of God.

This "bond of love" which joins the Father and man has also been contemplated by the Pope in the parable of the Prodigal Son (cf. Ch. 4). There the natural biological relationship of the earthly father to his Prodigal Son is the analogy for the metaphysical relationship of God the Father to the man of every period. This relationship cannot therefore be lost by the sins of the Prodigal Son.

The analogy goes further however. The biological Father/Son relationship is a familial relationship which rests on begetting. This "flows from the substance of the Father" and because of his constant faithfulness to his fatherhood it is indissoluble (cf. *DiM* 5.5; 6.1; 6.3). Man's unheard-of greatness consists in the basic value of his inviolable dignity of being a son!

But the offering of oneself to another is not simply begetting. That is why the devotion of God the Father to man as His created image need not necessarily be a begetting. According to the quoted text the Father has given man a participation "in the very life of God, Father, Son and Holy Ghost." According to this God's devotion to man can only mean that the Father gives himself to man as His created image *in the Son* and in this substantial union ("equally brought together") constitutes and calls into being the substance: man. This means that "Christ's being" is identical to "being in Christ" as the most profound being of every man. The eternally begotten Son would be the universal ontological principle of being of humanity. That explains the strong statement that it is the same love of the Father for man and for His only begotten Son on the cross; a love which is said to have called into existence man as the image and likeness of God. The Sonship would not just be "constitutive" for the relationship of the Father to His eternally begotten Son, the "figure of His substance" (Heb. 1:3), but also for the relationship of the Father to man, the "likeness of His substance." That is the case for every man *ab origine*, for the whole of humanity.

The particular in the teaching on the Redemption in the Encyclical shows itself when it is compared with the New Testament and classical theology:

According to Sacred Scripture the fruit of the Redemption is to become a true child of God, "Behold what manner of charity the Father hath bestowed upon us, that we should be called, and should be the sons of God" (I Jn. 3:1). In St. Paul it is written of God, "(I) will be a Father to you; and you shall be my sons and daughters" (II Cor. 6:18). God makes Himself a gift and according to Jesus' words dwells in the disciples, "If any one love me, he will keep my word, and my Father will love him, and we will come to him, and will make our abode with him" (Jn. 14:23). Through this, according to the words of the Lord, there will be a "perfect unity" in Christ,

> That they all may be one, as thou, Father, in me, and I in thee; that they also may be one in us; that the world may believe that thou hast sent me. And the glory which thou hast given me, I have given to them; that they may be one, as we also are one: I in them, and thou in me; that they may be made perfect in one (Jn. 17:21-23).

The new being of a Christian is then a "being in Christ." From the many places in St. Paul we give here just one example, "The grace of God is life everlasting, in Christ Jesus our Lord" (Rom. 6:23). The Christian's new principle of life is the Holy Ghost, who proceeds from the Father and the Son and is sent into our hearts. Thus is the Epistle to the Romans

(5:5) we read, "The charity of God is poured forth in our hearts, by the Holy Ghost, who is given to us" (Rom. 5,5). Further, "You have received the spirit of adoption of sons, whereby we cry: Abba (Father)" (Rom. 8:15). We are the temple of the Holy Ghost (I Cor. 3:16), "Know you not, that you are the temple of God, and that the Spirit of God dwelleth in you?" We have been made "partakers of the divine nature" (II Pet. 1:4) and have therefore in Christ a participation in the trinitarian life of God.—But this is all said of the believing Christian, not just for any man.

The fathers, following the example of Holy Scripture, have stressed the dignity of being a child of God. Thus St. Augustine says, "That is why God became man that man may become God."[17] Classical theology does not just speak of an unheard-of dignity but even of the "divine dignity in which man participates because of being made a member of Christ."[18]

But Adam's descendants do not possess the fruits of the incarnation and Redemption *ab origine* in such a way that they cannot lose them. Rather Christ earned these fruits through His historical work of salvation, they were offered to man in Original Sin, also in history and they are applied in the process of justification.[19] It is a fundamental truth in the New Testament that the grace of being a child of God must be "accepted" by a man in the faith. It is only to those who received the *Logos* to whom He "gave...power to be made the sons of God, to them that believe in his name" (Jn. 1:12).

In the fathers, too, the "participation in the divine nature" (II Pet. 1:4) is the foundation for an inner "familial relationship" between God and man.[20] Classical theology has been very careful in explaining exactly what this relationship means.

---

17 "*Factus est Deus homo, ut homo fieret Deus*" (Serm. 13 de temp.).

18 Matthias Joseph Scheeben, *Die Mysterien des Christentums* [*The Mysteries of Christianity*] [= *Mysterien*] (Freiburg i. Br. 1951), collected writings II, pp. 312ff.

19 Matthias Joseph Scheeben, *Dogmatik, op. cit.* V/2, no. 1326-1342.

20 Matthias Joseph Scheeben, *Mysterien, op. cit.* p. 315.

At the centre are the terms God's image and likeness—just as in the Encyclical. Unfortunately the Pope in the Encyclical does not use any further scholastic distinctions to make these central concepts clearer, *e.g.*, nature and grace, actual and sanctifying grace, created and uncreated grace, *etc.* They are mocked by modern "immanence theology" as being representative of an unreliable "dualism." They do, however, show up the decisive point very clearly.

The decisive point is this: What does the participation of man as image and likeness of God in the divine nature mean?

According to classical teaching there are two extremes to be avoided in the way and manner of the participation of man in the divine nature:[21]

> a) It may not be understood in the *pantheistic* sense of a changing of the substance of the soul into the divinity. The infinite distance between Creator and creature remains intact (D. 433, 510, 1225).
>
> b) It may also not be understood merely as a *moral* participation with God which consists in the imitation of the moral perfections of God, analogous to the sinner's being a child of the devil (Jn. 8:44).
>
> c) Positively it is a *physical* participation of man in God. This consists in an *accidental* union which happens by a created gift of God making the soul like to God and uniting it in a way which goes beyond all created power. Man, who by nature is a *vestigium Dei,* his body being the embodiment of a divine idea, is an *imago Dei,* his spirit being an image of the divine Spirit. He becomes a *similitudo Dei, i.e.,* a higher, supernatural degree of likeness to God through sanctifying grace.

With this background the differences in what the Pope teaches about the Redemption can be clearly seen:

The participation of man in the divine nature is a physical one in the Encyclical also. It consists, however, not in an acci-

[21] Ludwig Ott, *op. cit.* p. 296.—Concerning "sanctifying grace" this is only dealt with in *Dominum et Vivificantem.*

dental but in a *substantial* union. The participation in the divine nature is not sanctifying grace (*gratia creata*) which makes the natural image of God in man a supernatural likeness of the uncreated beauty of God, changing it according to the image of the Son of God (Rom. 8:29; Gal. 4:19), making it like God and so uniting it with God according to its quality (=accidentally). It is rather God Himself (*gratia increata*) who unites Himself in the act of Creation immediately and substantially with His created image and makes it thereby a consubstantial likeness and in this way creates the substance of man as His image and likeness "on an equal footing." Christ's being and "being in Christ" of every man are thus substantially identical. Is that not a pantheistic misinterpretation of man's being a child of God?

Since in the Encyclical God's image and likeness constitute man's nature, being God's child is something you cannot lose. Man finds himself basically redeemed. The grace of being God's child is therefore not given to the individual due to his faith and baptism, that is, in the course of history in the process of justification. Being God's child is said to belong indeed *ab origine* to man's nature.

Thus the centre of the Pope's theory of God's inviolable covenant of grace with man *ab origine* should now be clear and we can now see why the Father gives over His Son for the restoration of God's objectively required justice so that He can perform satisfaction to the faithfulness of the Father to this covenant for the sins of men.

7.5 God's wonderful covenant with man

God's giving of Himself to man is the foundation of a holy community of love. We read (*DiM* 7.5):

> The cross of Christ on Calvary stands beside the path of that *admirabile commercium*, of that wonderful self-communication of God to man, which also includes the call to man to share in the divine life by giving himself, and with himself

the whole visible world, to God, and like an adopted son to become a sharer in the truth and love which is in God and proceeds from God.

Christ's cross on Calvary which stands "beside" that *admirabile commercium* is therefore just a "wayside cross" only a sign of that more profound inviolable union of God and man.

That *commercium* is understood significantly as an "invitation" to man to answer God's giving of Himself by the giving of his own self. The acceptance of this invitation can obviously be ignored without man's ontological relationship of being a child of God being lost. Man would then not reach the "fullness" of life which proceeds from God in this life (cf. *DiM* 7.3).

The Pope uses the concept of adoptive son this time to describe the relationship of being a child taking it from the letters of St. Paul and the Church's teaching on grace (Rom. 8:15 & 23; Gal. 4:5; Eph. 1:5). In the Latin text it says literally, Man participates in God's life in the manner of an adoptive son (*more adoptivi filii consors*).

In the New Testament adoptive sonship is the same as being a child of God (cf. Rom. 8:15-17; Gal. 4:5ff.; Jn. 1:12; I Jn. 3:1 & 2 & 9).

The essential has already been said in this matter (cf. above *DiM* 7.4). We will just go over the controversial point.

According to Church teaching man becomes an adoptive child of God through justification. This process is described by the Council of Trent: Man is taken from the state in which he is born as a son of the First Adam by the Second Adam Jesus Christ our Saviour and put into a state of grace and adoption as a son of God (D 796). This removal (translation) from the state of Original Sin to the state of an adoptive son of God takes place due to the faith and the bath of rebirth (D 796ff.). In the New Testament the adoptive sonship is understood in the sense of an analogical generation (Jn. 1:13; 3:3ff.). The example is of course the eternal generation of Christ's sonship.[22]

The concept of adoptive sonship from Scripture and Church teaching has another specific meaning in the Encyclical: Here adoptive sonship means the adoption of every man as the created image of God in the act of Creation to whom the Father has given Himself *actu uno* as a gift and therefore makes in His likeness as an adoptive son.

As the Pope made his exegesis of the Old and New Testament finally become part of his theology of the covenant so it happens for the third time in the Paschal mystery (*DiM* 7.5):

> It is precisely beside the path of man's eternal election to the dignity of being an adopted child of God that there stands in history the cross of Christ (*Ita plane secundum viam aeternae hominis destinationis ad filii Dei adoptivi dignitatem eminet in historia crux Christi*), the only-begotten Son, who, as "light from light, true God from true God," came to give the final witness to the wonderful covenant of God with humanity, of God with man—every human being. This covenant, as old as man—it goes back to the very mystery of Creation—and afterwards many times renewed with one single chosen people, is equally the new and definitive covenant, which was established there on Calvary, and is not limited to a single people, to Israel, but is open to each and every individual.

The cross of Christ stands once again just "beside the path," this time "beside the path of man's eternal election to the dignity of being an adopted child." This means in effect the predestination of the whole of humanity to this dignity in the act of Creation. Because the dignity of an adoptive son belongs to the nature of man as God's image and likeness it is also inviolable.

The following review of the Pope's theology of the covenant is as it were the theological key to the teaching of universal salvation which summarises all preceding statements. With a

---

[22] *Ibid.* pp. 71ff.

few words the Pope announces his new teaching:

According to it the cross is the "last witness" (*novissimum testimonium*) of the eternal, wonderful covenant of grace which God has made with Adam, the whole of humanity, with "every man" *actu uno* at the Creation. This covenant with Adam and humanity, which contains the eternal election and inviolable adoptive sonship of every man "is as it were the new and eternal covenant which was made on Calvary." The covenant with Adam is thus substantially identical with the new and everlasting covenant of Calvary. The cross of Christ is just "the last witness" to this covenant which since Adam is the continual and intact foundation of the whole history of salvation and humanity. The double bond which since the Creation binds God as Creator and Father with man, His image and likeness, has never been broken, not even by Original Sin, because it is indissoluble due to the Father's giving of Himself to man and His absolute faithfulness to His fatherhood.[23]

Holy Scripture, however, says nothing about such a wonderful covenant of grace with man. The Encyclical is a closed presentation of the Pope's theory of universal salvation. It has, however, no foundation in Holy Scripture nor in the Church's teaching.

7.6 The last word of God's covenant and the new faith

Finally the Encyclical turns to the glorious side of the Paschal mystery (*DiM* 7.6):

> What else, then, does the cross of Christ say to us, the cross that in a sense is the final word of His messianic message and mission? And yet this is not yet the word of God of the covenant: that will be pronounced at the dawn when first the women and then the Apostles come to the tomb of the crucified Christ, see the tomb empty and for the first time hear the message, "He is risen." They will repeat this message

[23] Cf. Part II/1, pp. 24-32.

> to the others and will be witnesses to the risen Christ. Yet, even in this glorification of the Son of God, the cross remains, that cross which—through all the messianic testimony of the Son of Man, who suffered death upon it—speaks and never ceases to speak of God the Father, who is absolutely faithful to His eternal love for man, since He "so loved the world"—therefore man in the world—that "he gave his only Son, that whoever believes in him should not perish but have eternal life" (Jn. 3:16).

The cross is therefore "in a sense" the last word of the Messiah, but not of God's covenant. The last word of God's covenant is the Resurrection. Why this strange split in Christ's work of Redemption?

When the cross is "a word of the Messiah" then surely the Resurrection also! As Christ's death on the cross is the meritorious cause of our Redemption so Christ's resurrection is the victorious perfection of the work of Redemption. Cross and Resurrection form together the completeness of the work of Redemption and are presented in Holy Scripture as one thing (cf. Rom. 4:25).[24]

The Encyclical does describe insistently how the cross in the glorification of the Son of God "never ceases to speak of the Father." But there is no mention of the continuation of the Risen One's work of Redemption. It is simply cut off by the Encyclical taking away as it were this "last word" and declaring the Resurrection to be simply the "last word of God's covenant...who is absolutely faithful to His love for man." In this way the Resurrection is transposed into the Pope's new theology of the covenant: The Resurrection is thus made a witness of God's covenant for His indissoluble covenant of grace with man *ab origine* with everything which this covenant includes. The "last word of God's covenant" is thus the universal giving of grace which is manifested in Christ's resur-

---

[24] Cf. Matthias Joseph Scheeben, *Dogmatik, op. cit.* V/2, no. 1278.

rection!

Whereas, in the New Testament and Church teaching, the Resurrection is the objective completion of Christ's work of Redemption: the sealing of it and its formal and solemn ratification. In the Resurrection Christ reveals the power of His divinity which is the condition for His power of redeeming.

The Resurrection is the pledge of the eternally valid effectiveness of Christ's work of Redemption. For this is transformed through the Resurrection into an eternal state of living presentation before God. The Resurrection is Christ's perfection as an intermediary between God and man who as high priest and glorified victim continues for ever His rôle as intercessor and saviour. It is the Risen One Himself who applies the fruits of His merited reparation to each individual, frees him from the hopeless state of Original Sin and every personal sin because of his faith and penance, justifies him and reconciles him to God.

The Resurrection is finally the example of the effects which Christ has earned through His work of Redemption. The Risen One's heavenly life which comes from Christ's death shows the redeemed believer that he too can and should enjoy a similar heavenly life of body and soul because of the death of Christ.[25]

The revelation of the Paschal mystery corresponds on man's side to faith. This time the Encyclical uses the full quotation (as in text above) from the Gospel according to St. John with the condition of faith (3, 16) but gives straight away what should be understood by faith (*DiM* 7.6):

> Believing in the crucified Son means "seeing the Father," (cf. Jn. 14:9) means believing that love is present in the world and that this love is more powerful than any kind of evil in which individuals, humanity, or the world are involved. Believing in this love means believing in mercy. For mercy is an indispensable dimension of love; it is as it were love's second

[25] *Ibid.*

> name and, at the same time, the specific manner in which love is revealed and effected *vis-à-vis* the reality of the evil that is in the world, affecting and besieging man, insinuating itself even into his heart (*animum*) and capable of causing him to "perish in Gehenna" (Mt. 10:28).

According to this "faith" means to believe everything which the Pope has said so far about divine mercy and the Redemption. This "faith" is naturally not the same as the faith of the New Testament.[26]

The last sentence of the quoted text reaches its climax with a quotation threatening Hell. The quotation is the impressive conclusion of the whole article. At the same time it begs the question: How can we reconcile "perishing in Hell" with the carefully developed theory of universal salvation? The expectation that this question will be answered in the next article which deals fundamentally with the problem of evil in the world is however disappointed. There is no more mention of Gehenna. This quotation from Scripture is not taken up. It is just there as a stylistic feature.

8. The Paschal mystery and the reality of evil *

After presenting the cross and Resurrection as a sign of God's indissoluble covenant of grace with man (*DiM* 7), the Pope builds his vision of the history of salvation on this foundation, dressed up in biblical and traditional language, concerning the Paschal mystery considering the reality of evil in the world (*DiM* 8).

8.1 The cross: "Sign of the power of evil against the Son of God"

The Pope begins once again with the sorrowful side of the

---

[26] Cf. Part I, pp. 108-118.

* Article title in English translation, "Love More Powerful Than Death, More Powerful Than Sin."

Paschal mystery.

The Encyclical says about the person of the Crucified (*DiM* 8.1):

> The cross of Christ on Calvary is also a sign of the power of evil against the very Son of God (*Praeterea Christi crux in Calvariae loco testimonium pariter de mali potentia contra ipsum Filium Dei*), against the one who, alone among all the sons of men, was by His nature absolutely innocent and free from sin, and whose coming into the world was untainted by the disobedience of Adam and the inheritance of Original Sin.

If the cross of Christ on Calvary was up till now "the witness of the wonderful covenant of God with man" (cf. *DiM* 7.5), now it is "also a sign of the power of evil against the very Son of God."

The cross as witness of the universal giving of grace is the fundamental presupposition for the consideration of the cross as witness of the power of evil. This last is the key to the covenant of grace *ab origine.*

The Pope begins his consideration in the middle of the conflict between good and evil. Holy Scripture understands the phrase "power of evil" as something personal. Thus Satan and the Son of God stand in terrible confrontation. To how this battle ends the Encyclical says: "Look to the Cross"!

"The cross is the sign of the power of evil against the very Son of God" (*contra ipsum Filium Dei*).

The cross as a proof (*testimonium*) of the might of Satan against the Son of God is a terrible sight! A consequence which was certainly not foreseen by the author. It is however completely in harmony with what has previously been said: A Messiah who in His Passion expects mercy and release from men, who pleads in vain for the Father's mercy (cf. *DiM* 7.2 & 3), is now on the cross the proof of Satan's power against Him!

This is modern "Christology from below"! The external-experimental, human-historical event controls the way things are viewed. But already for the "high priests together with the scribes and elders" Christ on the cross was a "proof" of the falseness of His claims (cf. Mt. 27:39-44). But the cross, for the Jews a scandal and for the pagans foolishness is grace and wisdom of God which can only be understood by the revelation of God (cf. I Cor. 1:18-29).

The Lord Himself, looking ahead to His Passion, gives the definitive answer to what the Encyclical says, "The prince of this world cometh, *and in me he hath not any thing*" (Jn. 14:30).

The cross is therefore not at all a sign of the power of Satan against the very Son of God.

The power of Satan, so the Encyclical goes on, shows itself against Him who alone by His nature was absolutely free from sin, "was untainted by the disobedience of Adam and the inheritance of Original Sin." With these words the relationship of the cross to Original Sin is stated.

From what the Encyclical says it follows that apart from Jesus Christ all other men are by their nature not free from the disobedience of Adam, from Original Sin and from personal sin. Does this clear statement mean a contradiction to what has been so positively affirmed about the thesis of universal salvation? Not at all. Because this says that all other men—just like the Immaculate[27]—"from grace" enter existence free from Original Sin as redeemed and justified (cf. *DiM* 7.4). What is said in the quoted text is formulated from the point of view of universal salvation with no shadow of contradiction and must be understood in this way. The problem of the Encyclical is that man has an indissoluble union in grace with God—in spite of his sins.

Seen from the point of view of classical theology one would expect that, in an article which fundamentally deals with the theme of evil in the world with reference to the Paschal mystery (*DiM* 8), Original Sin would be looked at first. For, according to the Church's teaching, Original Sin is the presup-

---

[27] Cf. *Redemptor Hominis* 13.3.

position for the Redemption through the cross. But in the Encyclical Original Sin has very little to do with it. The "inheritance of Original Sin" is only mentioned once in the quoted text and then not even with direct reference to man but to Christ. The reason is obvious: In a theology which is founded on the axiom of universal salvation man is essentially saved. That is why there can be nobody *in statu naturae lapsae* who would have to be redeemed by the cross of Christ and "brought into a state of grace and being an adopted son of God" (cf. D 796ff.). Which is why the sacrifice of the cross must necessarily undergo a change of meaning through the thesis of universal Redemption.

– The Encyclical has this to say about the sacrifice of the cross (*DiM* 8.1):

> And here, precisely in Him, in Christ, justice is done to sin at the price of His sacrifice, of His obedience "even unto death" (Phil. 2:8). He who was without sin, "God made him sin for our sake" (*Eum qui non noverat peccatum, "pro nobis peccatum fecit"*) (II Cor. 5:21). Justice is also brought to bear upon death, which from the beginning of man's history had been allied to sin (*sociata cum peccato est*). Death has justice done to it at the price of the death of the one who was without sin and who alone was able—by means of his own death—to inflict death upon death (cf. I Cor. 15:54).

The text seems to reflect the traditional teaching of the sacrifice of the Cross as a reparative offering made in our place.[28] But it must be understood in the context of the Encyclical:

According to this, the cross of Christ is first and foremost "the sign of the wonderful covenant of God" with universally redeemed humanity which can never be broken and is substantially identical with the "new and definitive covenant of Calvary" (cf. *DiM* 7.5).

[28] Cf. Ludwig Ott, *op. cit.*, pp. 217ff.

This means that in the Pope's teaching of universal salvation there is absolutely no historical work of Redemption of Christ in the sense of the New Testament since man is saved ab origine. *This fundamental novelty must be clearly understood if what the Encyclical says about the sacrifice of the cross is to be properly understood.*

In the quoted text the sacrifice of the cross is thus not the work of Redemption which has saved man in Original Sin from his hopeless state and reconciled him with God—in the sense of traditional belief. The cross is on the contrary first of all the witness to the universal giving of grace to man who has an indissoluble covenant of grace with God *ab origine*. In the sense of this covenant of grace Christ's sacrifice on the cross is not a "redemptive sacrifice" in the sense of Holy Scripture but only a sacrifice of reparation for the sins of man who has been universally redeemed *a priori*.

This specific reparative character of the sacrifice of the cross can be defined more precisely. The Pope's fundamental theory of the doctrine of Redemption is: The Father gave up the Son and "made him a sin for us" so that He may perform satisfaction for the faithfulness of the Father to His covenant of grace with universally redeemed man for the sins of man (cf. *DiM* 7.1). This constant faithfulness has an ontological reason: God as Creator and Father is bound physically and substantially, therefore indissolubly, by the act of Creation and giving of Himself to man, His image and likeness. For the Father's giving of Himself to man in the act of Creation is part of man's nature (cf. 7.4). But because of His holiness and justice God has to require satisfaction for man's sins. That is why the Father makes the son "a sin for us" and hands Him over in our place to His reparative death. The sacrifice of the cross is therefore *only* a sacrifice of reparation. Its specific character of reparation consists *only* of being satisfaction for the Father's faithfulness to His covenant of grace and for the inviolable dignity of being a son which He gave to man along with grace, even though and because man still sins. Christ dies therefore on the cross not for a sinner in need of Redemption but for a man who possesses an inviolable supernatural dignity of being a son.

The character of reparation of the sacrifice of the cross can be defined more clearly by comparing it with traditional teaching: In the Church's teaching Redemption by the sacrifice of the cross means negatively being freed from sin and positively being reconciled with God which includes the whole riches of God's covenant of grace. In the Encyclical the positive side is obviously missing. Man has already a covenant of grace with God (cf. *DiM* 7). Thus the negative side which is left is also reinterpreted. The sacrifice of the cross is not to free man from Original Sin and his personal sins but only a reparation for God's offended holiness and justice. The Father's love for man is shown by His making the Son "a sin for us" and letting Him be punished for us in our place.

This specific character of reparation of the sacrifice of the cross has another aspect which we find in the quoted text where the whole argumentation is based on the sentence, "The cross of Christ on Calvary is also a sign of the power of evil against the very Son of God." This statement is continued, "and precisely in Him" justice is done to sin and death. According to this the cross as a sacrifice of reparation is also a "witness of Satan's might."

It thus follows quite logically that it is Satan's power which forces Christ to be crucified. The Father appears as the one who, out of faithfulness to His covenant of grace with man, "makes for us a sin" the Son who begs for mercy and is handed over—*horribile est dictu*—to the power of Satan as a reparation for our sins. Then the Son would have had to submit Himself to the power of Satan out of obedience to the Father, the Father would have had to accept the sacrifice of one driven by the power of Satan to death on the cross as reparation. This consequence is not so clearly visible in the quoted text because it is dressed up in biblical language.

Thus we must continue to ask the urgent question about

the power of evil against the very Son of God—this time as a diabolical power in the atoning sacrifice of the Son. For the believing Christian it can only be answered by looking in Holy Scripture itself.

In the Gospels the confrontation of the Son of God with the power of evil is a central theme of the messianic mission of Christ: For "the Son of God appeared, that he might destroy the works of the devil" (I Jn. 3:8).

The open conflict begins immediately at the beginning of the messianic ministry of Christ—with the Temptation. The power of evil *in persona* against the Son of God *in persona* is shown to be completely powerless (cf. Mt. 4:1-11). Before His Passion Christ declares, "For the prince of this world cometh, and in me he hath not any thing. But that the world may know, that I love the Father: and as the Father hath given me commandment, so do I" (Jn. 14:30ff.). In these clear words of our Lord the cross is neither a proof of the power of Satan against the very Son of God nor of the power of Satan in the work of Redemption. Rather the cross is the proof of the Son's love for the Father and His obedience in fulfilling His commands.

What does the power of Satan actually have to do with the final fulfilment of these commands—in Gethsemane, in the Passion, on the cross? Christ Himself says to the band in the Garden, "but this is your hour, and the power of darkness" (Lk. 22:53). The obvious proof for the "power of darkness" seems to be given by the Passion that follows.

Jesus describes the character of this "power of darkness" against the Son of God before Pilate, the representative of the pagan Roman world power, before His Passion, "Thou shouldst not have any power against me unless it were given thee from above" (Jn. 19:11). The power from above is God. Thus it is God Himself who hands over His Son to this power and "delivered him up for us all" (Rom. 8:32). Rome's power is a real historical power but it is given by God, dependent, permitted. Pilate is but the instrument in the hand of divine providence when he delivers the Son of God over to be crucified in his own name.[29]

But the fate of Christ is "not decided by human will but by divine power."[30] The sacrifice of the cross is decided only by the the inner workings of the divine will, as it is greatly emphasised in the New Testament and the Church's teaching.

What the Father does in "making for us a sin" the Son and handing Him over to the power of evil would be actually an arbitrary and unjust thing to do if the Son Himself had not freely and in perfect love to the Father and us men fulfilled the Father's will and taken on the punishment of suffering as reparation for our sins.[31]

This inner decision of the Son's loving and free self-giving decides also the character of His obedience, "unto death on the cross" (Phil. 2:8). It is man's sin that Christ brings to the cross and for which He does reparation. But that is no reason why the sacrifice of the cross is a proof of the power of evil against Christ. For by using all his power and aiming at the destruction of the Son of God, Satan, as the simple tool of divine providence, due to the loving obedience of the Son even unto death, prepares his own defeat. In this way the great humiliation of Christ on the cross becomes in reality His greatest triumph over the power of evil. The absolutely free obedience unto death is the most radical defeat of sin. In the quoted text there is a reference to Phil. 2:8 but this is just a quotation in the context of the Encyclical and therefore hides the fact that in the context of St. Paul's letter to the Philippians (Phil. 2:6ff.) it is precisely the Redeemer's free loving giving of himself which determines the character of the sacrifice of the cross.

The sacrifice of the cross cannot be seen merely in the context of the Father's act of salvation, for "all external acts of

---

[29] Hermann Strathmann, *Das Evangelium nach Johannes* [*The Gospel According to John*] (Göttingen 1963), NTD IV, p. 237.

[30] Rudolf Bultmann, *Theologie des Neuen Testaments* [*Theology of the New Testament*] (Tübingen 1966, 6th edition), p. 396.

[31] Matthias Joseph Scheeben, *Dogmatik, op. cit.* V/2, no. 1304.

God are common to all Three Persons": (D 428; 704), the work of Redemption included.[32] But only the Son became man and performed the work of Redemption as a medium between God and man. Not only did the Father give the Son for us but also the Son "delivered himself for us" (Gal. 2:20). The Father's giving of the Son is related to the Son's giving of Himself. We must see both sides. The Son is not just a passive victim but also the Priest of the sacrifice Himself.

– Concerning the effect of the sacrifice of the cross in history the Encyclical says (*DiM* 8.1):

> In this way the cross of Christ, on which the Son, consubstantial with the Father, renders full justice to God (*plenam retribuit Deo iustitiam*), is also a radical revelation of mercy, or rather of the love that goes against what constitutes the very root of evil in the history of man: against sin and death.

According to this the cross of Christ is the full satisfaction for the offended justice of the Father, *i.e.,* merely reparation. The Son did this once and for all in abundance on Calvary (cf. *DiM* 7.3). After the sacrifice of the cross is reduced to an act of reparation the cross of Christ confronted with evil in history remains merely a *function* of a "radical revelation" of merciful love which goes against the root of all evil.

Thus the Pope begins his presentation of the foundation of his consideration and sketches the scheme of his history of salvation. In a subtle formulation he shifts the points for his view of salvation: It is not the sacrifice of the cross itself which goes against the very root of evil but the radical revelation of love which is a result of the cross.

According to the Church's teaching it is nonetheless the sacrifice of the cross itself which not only goes against (*adversatur*) the root of all evil with the full force of its redeeming reality but rips out this root by the Redeemer wiping out Original

[32] Ludwig Ott, *op. cit.* pp. 179ff.

Sin and all personal sins in the process of justification, reconciling the penitent sinner with God, putting him in a state of grace and of being an adoptive son and giving him a participation in the fullness of grace of the Redemption (D 793-800). Faith, baptism and Church are in this process necessary for salvation (*necessitas medii*). According to Scripture death is not only linked to sin from the beginning of man's history but "death is the wages of sin" (Rom 6:23), *i.e.,* a punishment.

With the background of the Church's teaching it becomes clear what the Encyclical completely leaves out when dealing with the confrontation of the sacrifice of the cross with evil in history because man is already *a priori* universally in a state of grace.

8.2 The cross of Christ and evil in the history of man

How the cross of Christ as revelation of merciful love goes against evil in history is described in the following text (*DiM* 8.2):

> The cross is the most profound condescension of God to man and to what man (*Crux ergo humillima inclinatio Divinitatis est super hominem*)—especially in difficult and painful moments—looks on as his unhappy destiny. The cross is like a touch of eternal love upon the most painful wounds of man's earthly existence (*Crux autem quasi amoris aeterni contrectatio est vulnerum acerrime dolentium in terrena vita*); it is the total fulfilment of the messianic programme that Christ once formulated in the synagogue at Nazareth (Lk. 4:18-21) and then repeated to the messengers sent by John the Baptist (Lk. 7:20-23). According to the words once written in the prophecy of Isaiah (Is. 35:5; 61:1-3), this programme consisted in the revelation of merciful love for the poor, the suffering and prisoners, for the blind, the oppressed and sinners.

This humanly impressive presentation is not just a pious supposition but the Pope's dogmatic statement in an Encyclical about the central object of the Christian religion.

Certainly the cross is the most profound condescension of God to what man looks on as his "unhappy destiny." But the cross says much more than what man himself considers as his misfortune: It reveals to him his true state before God as a sinner in absolute need of Redemption (Rom. 3:9ff.).

Certainly the cross is like a touch of love upon "wounds of man's earthly existence." But the sacrifice of the cross on Calvary is infinitely more: It heals the loss of his supernatural life and the wounds in his human nature left by Original Sin. The cross touches not only the most painful wounds of man but goes to his most inner being and makes him a "new Creation" (cf. II Cor. 5:17). Christ shed His blood not for our temporal well-being but for our eternal life.

Is this overlooked by the Pope? Not at all. He just has another theology of Redemption. According to this the cross is the "sign" of God's indissoluble covenant of grace with man (cf. *DiM* 7). If man is already *ab origine* in possession of the supernatural fruits of Redemption then the cross retains just the function of a sign of this state of salvation and the loving "touching" of the wounds of "man's earthly existence."

The consideration of the suffering in "man's earthly existence" culminates in the Encyclical's statement that the cross is "the total fulfilment of the messianic programme that Christ once formulated in the synagogue at Nazareth" (Lk. 4:18-21). It is, however, obvious that the total fulfilment of that programme would be the healing of all human needs and crimes, *i.e.,* the perfect restoration of an earthly paradise by the Messiah but not His death on the cross which put a definitive end to all Israel's messianic hopes. The aggressive refusal to believe and the synagogue's attempt to kill Christ because of what He claimed already show the road which leads to Calvary.[33] The cross is the "total fulfilment" of the refusal to believe.

---

[33] Karl Heinrich Rengstorf, *op. cit.* p. 69.

With the announcement of the messianic programme the Pope began his consideration (*DiM* 3.1). Just as in the first interpretation, the requirement to believe, which in the biblical text is indissolubly linked to the preaching of this programme, is abandoned. In this way the messianic programme is brought down to the level of the earthly life of man (cf. above *DiM* 3.8).

Certainly the revelation of God's merciful love found its final fulfilment in the cross but not in the sense of an earthly expectation for this life but in the sense of the Redemption from sin and the reconciliation with God. The kingdom of God is not of this world in the Gospel. Christ is not Mohammed.

– The next point of view from where the Pope looks at the function of the cross in history is the passage from death to life in the Paschal mystery. Here is what it says (*DiM* 8.2):

> In the Paschal mystery the limits of the many-sided evil in which man becomes a sharer during his earthly existence are surpassed: the cross of Christ, in fact, makes us understand (*perspiciamus*) the deepest roots of evil, which are fixed in sin and death; thus the cross becomes an eschatological sign. Only in the eschatological fulfilment and definitive renewal of the world will love conquer, in all the elect, the deepest sources of evil, bringing as its fully mature fruit the kingdom of life and holiness and glorious immortality. The foundation of this eschatological fulfilment is already contained in the cross of Christ and in His death (*Talis autem eschatologicae consummationis fundamentum in cruce iam Christi iacet ac morte*).

According to this the cross gives us simply the "knowledge" of "the deepest roots of evil" and the assertion that it will be overcome by love outside of history in the *Eschaton*.

But according to Scripture and Tradition the cross does not just let us "understand" the deepest roots of evil, it is rather the redemptive power which wipes out this root, *i.e.*, Original

Sin and personal sins in the justified person and gives to him that believes here and now eternal life. "He that believeth in the Son, hath life everlasting; but he that believeth not the Son, shall not see life; but the wrath of God abideth on him" (Jn. 3:36). That is why the cross is not the "eschatological sign" in the sense meant by the Encyclical that love only at the end of time will overcome "the deepest roots of evil." Through the cross they are overcome already in the believer!

It is obvious that the Encyclical understands something else dogmatically by "the deepest sources" or the "deepest roots" of evil from what Scripture and Tradition does. And it is here a matter of nothing less than the central object of Redemption.

Classical theology has put this point firmly in its place in the traditional teaching on the Redemption. This says that the first and immediate object of the Redemption (according to Rom. 5:12ff.) is the removal of man's general sin, *i.e.,* Original Sin and linked to that the restoration of supernatural justice as it was in the beginning but was lost by Adam's sin. The centre or substance of original justice is sanctifying grace. Because Original Sin is only a substantial impediment to the attaining of eternal salvation in so far as it includes the loss of sanctifying grace, Christ by no means had to add the gifts of integrity to the immediate and whole restoration of justice and original glory which he gave to the justified person with sanctifying grace. And as we can see, these gifts—freedom from disordered concupiscence, bodily immortality, freedom from suffering and subtility of knowledge—Christ did not and does not want to give us.[34]

The deficiencies which remain are part of human nature. But they do not have, for the justified person however, a character of guilt or punishment but simply the character of a necessity of nature which God did not want to suspend. They are brought into the service of the Redemption. By the prac-

[34] Matthias Joseph Scheeben, *Dogmatik, op. cit.,* V/2, no. 1327.

tise of virtue the justified person becomes like the Redeemer.[35] "For whether we live, we live unto the Lord; or whether we die, we die unto the Lord" (Rom 14:8).

Viewed from the standpoint of classical theology the character of this "deepest evil" of the Pope's teaching can be defined more clearly:

If man *ab origine* is in a state of grace, sin and death are not symptoms of being in Original Sin but merely of being a man which will be overcome in "the eschatological fulfilment." In this sense the cross is the "eschatological sign...of the definitive renewal of the world."

– The third view in which the Pope sees the function of the cross in a history marked by sin and death is the resurrection of Christ. He says (*DiM* 8.2):

> The fact that Christ "was raised the third day" (I Cor. 15:4), constitutes the final sign of the messianic mission, a sign that perfects the entire revelation of merciful love in a world that is subject to evil (*Postremeum officii messianici indicium, quod quidem revelationem cumulat misericordis amoris in mundo malis obnoxio*). At the same time it constitutes the sign (*Id eodem similiter tempore signum constituit*) that foretells "a new heaven and a new earth," (Apoc. 21:1) when God "will wipe away every tear from their eyes, there will be no more death, or mourning, or crying, nor pain, for the former things have passed away (Apoc. 21:4).

In the New Testament, however, the fact of the resurrection is more than just an "index" or "sign" that foretells a new heaven and a new earth. For Christ Himself the resurrection is the effective entrance into the state of glory as a reward for His humiliation in His suffering. For us the resurrection is not just the foretelling of a new world when history is over but the victorious climax of the work of Redemption which has brought forth a new Creation (Gal. 6:15) into the old order

---

[35] *Ibid.* no. 1328.

where everything was lost. Man participates in this here and now by faith and baptism (Rom. 6:3ff.). The Risen One is an example and pledge for this newly given supernatural reality in faith and for man's future bodily resurrection and the end of time (I Cor. 15:20ff.; Phil. 3:21).[36]

The Pope's vision of the history of salvation which rests on the foundation that everyone is given grace is something completely new:

In this new history of salvation there is no man who was in a state of being lost and in enmity with God, who would then have to be redeemed by the cross from the vale of the shadow of death and brought to a state of being a child of God. Christ's Incarnation, cross and resurrection are not God's unique eschatological act of salvation which breaks in on the hopeless old age and puts man in a state where he must make a decision of faith; putting an end to the old age and bearing a new Creation of grace from the waters of baptism which will be fulfilled in the *eschaton*. In the Pope's new history of salvation man's Redemption has lost its historical character. It is no longer a true historical Redemption because man is already *a priori* redeemed and justified. That is why there is absolutely no mention of Original Sin, faith nor baptism in the Encyclical when the Pope talks about the confrontation of the cross with evil in history.

The new conception of the history of salvation leads necessarily to a new definition of the Church's mission.

8.3 Christ's messianic programme—The Church's programme

Christ's messianic message is next declared to be the Church's programme (*DiM* 8.3):

> In the eschatological fulfilment mercy will be revealed as love, while in the temporal phase, in human history, which is

---

[36] *Ibid.* no. 1278.

> at the same time the history of sin and death, love must be revealed above all as mercy and must also be actualised as mercy.
>
> Christ's messianic programme, the programme of mercy, becomes the programme of His people, the programme of the Church. At its very centre there is always the cross, for it is in the cross that the revelation of merciful love attains its culmination. Until "the former things pass away" (cf. Apoc. 21:4), the cross will remain the point of reference for other words too of the Revelation of John, "Behold I stand at the door and knock; if anyone hears my voice and opens the door, I will come in and eat with him and he with me" (Apoc. 3:20). In a special way, God also reveals His mercy when He invites man to have "mercy" on His only Son, the Crucified One.

The Encyclical opposes time and the end of time and then gives them each the fitting form of love and mercy: in history marked by sin and death love reveals itself as mercy in the perfection, at the end of time mercy reveals itself as love. When this is applied to Christ's and the Church's programme we get:

Christ's messianic programme with its high point in the merciful love of the cross is also the the programme of the Church.

The Pope has already dealt with Christ's messianic programme from the second chapter onwards from various historical points of view. One would expect him to simply say that this programme with which we are now familiar is now said to be the programme of the Church. But that is not the case. He goes to the centre of the missionary programme and describes it with the Lord's image from the Apocalypse 3:20: the Crucified One is standing at the door and asking for mercy.

In the quoted text it is emphasised: Yes, it is God Himself who invites man to have mercy on "his crucified Son" who is standing at the door and asking to be let in! This unusual explanation of Apoc. 3:20 is, however, just the logical consequence of the principle of the reciprocity of mercy and the understanding of the messianic mission of Christ and the

Church which is derived from it: The Messiah, who pleaded in vain for mercy from man and His Father (cf. 7.2 & 3) and whose cross is the proof of the power of evil against the very Son of God, (*DiM* 8.1) now stands as the "crucified Son" before man's door and asks for mercy and to be let in.

8.4 Reciprocal mercy between man and the Son of God

The Pope goes further with his exegesis of Apoc. 3:20 by continuing (*DiM* 8.4):

> Christ, precisely as the Crucified One, is the Word that does not pass away (Mt. 24:35), and He is the one who stands at the door and knocks at the heart of every man (cf. Apoc. 3:20), without restricting his freedom, but instead seeking to draw from this very freedom love, which is not only an act of solidarity with the suffering Son of man, but also a kind of "mercy" shown by each one of us to the Son of the eternal Father. In the whole of this messianic programme of Christ, in the whole revelation of mercy through the cross, could man's dignity be more highly respected and ennobled, for, in obtaining mercy, he is in a sense the one who at the same time "shows mercy"?

The image from Apoc. 3:20 is once again a parable for the messianic programme of the loving mercy of Christ and the Church. The theologically decisive point is emphasised. Thus the Pope removes any remaining doubts:

Yes, it is the Word made flesh, who as the crucified Messiah stands before man's door and asks for mercy and to be let in. Yes, it is God made man Himself to whom man can and should show not only solidarity but also a "quite personal mercy." Accepting the crucified Redeemer is then a reciprocal act of mercy which man performs for God made man. The Encyclical also gives the reason why: Man's dignity is thereby "respected and ennobled." Is it divine?

The Pope's main idea of equality and reciprocity in mercy (cf. *DiM* 6.4; 7.2 & 3) is with cold logic applied here to the relationship of man and the Man God and even to the work of Redemption itself. We must, however, remember that "Redemption" has a different meaning in the Encyclical: The sacrifice of the cross thanks to the Pope's theory of universal giving of grace is not a redemptive sacrifice in the sense of the traditional teaching of the Church, but only an atoning sacrifice for the sins which the Son performed because of the Father's faithfulness to his covenant of grace with man (cf. *DiM* 8.1).

It is only in appearance that something obvious is being said when we read that, when Christ asks to be let in, He does not restrict man's freedom but seeks "to draw from this very freedom love."

It is the clear teaching of the Church that the *Logos* who created man with free will does not, as crucified Redeemer, force anyone to accept Him. Only a free choice can be a moral choice. But from this free choice which accepts the Redeemer or not (cf. Jn. 1:10ff.), which gives obedient faith or not, depends salvation or damnation (Mk. 16:16).

In the Encyclical, however, the crucified Man-God does not just ask to be let in but also for "mercy." It is the Father Himself who "invites man to have 'mercy' on His only Son, the Crucified One" (*DiM* 8.3). And that is not something obvious but shows a fundamentally new understanding of the Redemption and therefore of the Church's mission.

The programme of the Church derived from how Christ acted is precisely the programme of Her mission. The central challenge of the mission is now no longer, "Convert and believe in the Gospel!" (Mk. 1:15), but, "Have mercy on Christ, the Crucified One!" Instead of believing in Christ we must now have mercy on Him. The Church's mission would therefore consist in begging man to have mercy on Christ the Crucified One as Christ Himself did. In the context of the Encyclical the new type of mission and conversion may be represented thus: By preaching the merciful love of the Father which is made visible in the Son, the missionary Church seeks to awaken "that creative power in man" which is based on his substance of being an adoptive son of God in full freedom to loving mercy for the Crucified One (cf. *DiM* 7.3 & 4), so that man attains the fullness of divine life (cf. *DiM* 7.3). Thus the principle of reciprocity in mercy would thus be also the principle of the Church's mission. It is no longer a question of faith or baptism, Redemption or justification of sinners "because of faith in Jesus Christ" (cf. Rom. 3:21ff.), but of reciprocal mercy of universally redeemed man and Christ the Crucified One.

At the centre of the Pope's new teaching is Christ's image from Apoc. 3:20. But what does the New Testament really say?

The image of Christ standing before the door and knocking (Apoc. 3:20) comes from the letter to the community in Laodicea (Apoc. 3:14-22). There Christ, "who is called Amen" and the "beginning of the Creation" (Apoc. 3:14), is God—as in the Encyclical. But that is where the similarity ends.

The glorified Lord who rules the universe with God (Apoc. 3:21) turns to the Church in Laodicea with sharp criticism. Because they are lukewarm they will be rejected at the judgment just as one is disgusted by filthy water and spits it out of one's mouth. The call to conversion which is directed at the self-satisfied community in such a harsh way is in fact an expression of merciful love with which the Lord wants to shake these lukewarm Christians out of their apathy and bring them to their senses. Christ is the divine Lord and Judge of His community. His appearance to judge them is close at hand. That is the meaning of, "Be zealous therefore and do penance. Behold I stand at the gate, and knock." (Apoc. 3:19ff.). The image is a warning of the judgment; a last call to conversion and watchfulness. The judge is already at the door and is knocking! The image is also a source of consolation and promise for whoever takes the warning seriously and converts, "If any man shall hear my voice, and open to me the door, I will come in to him, and will sup with him, and he with me" (Apoc. 3:20).[37]

[37] Eduard Lohse, *Die Offenbarung des Johannes* [*The Revelation of St. John*] (Göttingen 1966), NTD XI, pp. 33ff.

The harsh threat of judgment at the Lord's *Parousia*, who is already standing at the door, His call to conversion and watchfulness, the promise of supping with Him if one converts are the New Testament's expressions of the merciful love of Christ for His community at Laodicea.

In the biblical context Christ's love for His own is completely different to how it is represented in the Encyclical: The Son of God stands at the door as judge not as a beggar. He does not ask man for mercy but threatens him with a harsh judgment. There is no reciprocity of mercy between the crucified Son of God and miserable man according to a principle of equality (cf. *DiM* 6.4) and no bowing down to "the dignity of man."

In Holy Scripture the Redemption alone is the sovereign eschatological act of God's salvation which has been expressed in infinite mercy even unto the death on the cross of the Son Himself (Phil. 2:6ff.), to save His creature, who has rebelled and therefore is now in sin's shadow of death, from his misery and to rejoice him with his divine life. It is the Gospel's good news that the Good Shepherd goes after the lost sheep, that the father receives his son with joy and prepares his celebratory meal. It is the Gospel's good news that all of heaven rejoices over the return of one sinner who believes, converts and does penance.

But the Pope's main idea of equality, of common experience and reciprocity of mercy: that the "man of every period" possesses an inviolable dignity of being God's adoptive son which is supposed to form the common experience of mercy with the father (cf. *DiM* 6.4), that the father remains united in constant faithfulness to his covenant of grace with man who is universally redeemed *ab origine* and therefore hands His son over to an atoning death in order to invite man to have mercy on His only Son, the Crucified One, is with the best will in the world not to be found anywhere in the New Testament and certainly not in Apoc. 3:14ff.

In the Encyclical the messianic programme of mutual mercy

between man and God made man is nothing less than a whole new understanding of the Church's mission based on the theory of the universal giving of grace. The radical opposition to Christ's mission command is obvious (cf. Mk. 16:15ff.).

8.5 "The easy law of the plan of salvation"

The messianic programme of mutual mercy is the easy law of the plan of salvation. This is what the Pope has to say (*DiM* 8.5):

> In a word, is not this the position of Christ with regard to man when He says, "As you did it to one of the least of these...you did it to me" (Mt. 25:40)? Do not the words of the Sermon on the Mount, "Blessed are the merciful, for they shall obtain mercy" (Mt. 5:7) constitute, in a certain sense, a synthesis of the whole of the Good News, of the whole of the "wonderful exchange" (*admirabile commercium*) contained therein? This exchange is a law of the very plan of salvation, a law which is simple, strong and at the same time "easy." Demonstrating from the very start what the "human heart" is capable of ("to be merciful"), do not these words from the Sermon on the Mount reveal in the same perspective the deep mystery of God: that inscrutable unity of Father, Son and Holy Ghost, in which love, containing justice, sets in motion mercy, which in its turn reveals the perfection of justice?

The text is a masterpiece of the Pope's artistic skill. Apparently unpretentious and yet with the authority of an Encyclical, the reciprocal mercy between man and Christ, the Crucified One (cf. *DiM* 8.4) is with the added "justification" of biblical quotations raised to a general law and in the end founded on the Trinity. In the elusive form of a question the Pope makes Christ Himself as it were declare his main idea of equality and reciprocity in mercy an "easy law of the plan of salvation." In this way one of the Pope's favourite philosophical ideas is brought to the centre of the history of salvation by Christ Himself and made a decisive part of the plan of salvation.

The three questions in the quoted text contain three theses which are meant to justify and deepen the principle of equality and reciprocity each time using Holy Scripture. The theses are:

– Christ's actions and words show according to Mt. 25:40 the equality and reciprocity of mercy between man and Christ the Crucified One.

– The words of the Sermon on the Mount (Mt. 5:7) are a synthesis of the whole Gospel, of the "wonderful exchange" which marks the "gentle law of the plan of salvation" announced by Christ Himself.

– The words of the Sermon on the Mount (Mt. 5:7) also reveal the inscrutable unity of Father, Son and Holy Ghost.

The argumentation relies at each point on Holy Scripture. But is this done justly?

– The image from Apoc. 3:20 forms the theological centre of the messianic programme of reciprocal mercy: Christ stands before the door and asks for mercy (cf. *DiM* 8.3 & 4).

As further proof for this thesis Christ's words are used, "What you have done for the least of my brethren that you have done for me" (Mt. 25:40).

This quotation seems to justify the thesis: Christ, who in His whole life has shown mercy to man, now seems Himself to be in His brethren in need "personally" the receiver of man's mercy. At the same time using Mt. 25:40 the meeting of man and Christ, the Crucified One, takes place exclusively on the plane of merciful love. In the biblical parable of the Last Judgment (Mt. 25:31-46) mercy alone is the yardstick for judgment. Faith is not mentioned. This quotation seems to back up what the Pope is saying.

If man is *ab origine* saved then man's confrontation with the cross is not about the justification of sinners because of their faith in Jesus Christ (Rom. 3:22) but only about reciprocal mercy. It only remains for Christ's messianic programme and that of the Church to heal the "wounds of man's earthly existence" (cf. *DiM* 8.2).

That Mt. 25:40 should support the Encyclical's thesis, however, is only apparent. For just as Christ the Crucified One did not stand at man's door pleading for mercy in Apoc. 3:20 so neither in Mt. 25:40. In Apoc. 3:20 Christ threatens judgment at His *Parousia* and in Mt. 25:40 Christ is holding the Last Judgment at His *Parousia*. There is simply no equality and reciprocity in mercy between man and his divine Judge.

In the context of Holy Scripture Christ's words: "What you have done for the least of my brethren, that you have done for me" (Mt. 25:40) mean the works of mercy. They are what decides the Last Judgment. Christ puts Himself with His "least brethren." To the surprise of the just and the unjust alike the Judge declares that in the final reckoning He Himself was the recipient of these works of mercy.[38]

The decisive point in this judgment is that Christ applies the works of mercy which have been shown or not shown to those in need to Himself. This happens without those concerned knowing. This application by Christ of the works of mercy to Himself is, however, no proof of the thesis of equality and reciprocity of mercy between man and Christ the Crucified One. The distance between man and his divine Judge remains quite clearly:

In the Son of man's judgment He is obviously not identical to His "brother in need." He is his "brother." There is no equality. There is also no reciprocity: for the mercy shown to the "brother" in need is not returned by him at all. It is repaid by the Son of Man by the merciful reception into the Kingdom of Heaven. The one who showed mercy to his fellow man receives the mercy of the divine judge. Mercy isn't given reciprocally from equal to equal but goes one way, from above downwards: from the Son of Man to the just and from the just to the man in need. The relation to the Son of man is of an

[38] Julius Schniewind, *op. cit.* pp. 251-254.—Karl Staab, *op. cit.*, pp. 137-140.

indirect, moral nature. In the Last Judgment what is important is the yardstick for human acts not equality and reciprocity between the divine judge and man.

By using Mt. 25:40 as support for its thesis the Encyclical makes a mistake about what is being discussed. This was supposed to be the confrontation of man with Christ the Crucified One in the missionary activity of the Church *i.e.,* in history and not at the Last Judgment. It shouldn't need to be discussed that in the New Testament what Christ wants in His mission is the challenge to believe. In this diacritic confrontation, the Son of God does not ask man for mercy but demands with divine authority Faith (Mk. 16:15ff.). It is through faith in Christ the Crucified One that man receives justification from God (cf. Rom. 3:22). Faith on the other hand proves itself by works of charity which then decide whether one enters Heaven or not.

– In the second of the Encyclical's theses there is once again the use of Christ's words in the preconceived idea of equality and reciprocity in mercy.

Mt. 25:40 is deliberately dealt with first. For that quotation seems more than most to justify the principle of equality and reciprocity in mercy if one forgets what the Faith says. Mt. 25:40 is thus the basis for the generalisation of the principle which is followed by the second thesis, once again using Christ's words:

The words from the Sermon on the Mount, "Blessed are the merciful for they will obtain mercy" (Mt. 5:7) is now "a synthesis of the whole of the Good News." This synthesis is to be understood Christologically as the "wonderful exchange" in the sense of Mt. 25:40, *i.e.,* as reciprocal mercy between merciful man and Christ who makes Himself a companion of those in need. That is how it can be said that this exchange marks the plan of salvation as an "easy law."

In the New Testament these words of Christ from the Sermon on the Mount (Mt. 5:7) are a beatitude of human behaviour which comes from the Gospel. An ethical postulation is not the "whole Good News,"nor the work of Redemption. The concrete sense of the beatitude is given by Jesus in the parable of unmerciful servant (Mt. 18:21-35): Because God in His mercy has forgiven us our huge debt we must also be merciful to those who owe us lesser debts. This is the same as in the Our Father, "Forgive us our trespasses as we forgive them that trespass against us." The *analogia entis* is clear. The idea of a mutual forgiving of sins between God and man would be absurd.

In the New Testament the "synthesis of the whole Gospel" is Christ Himself. According to Mk. 1:1 the Gospel is the Good News of Jesus Christ the Son of God. The Good News also includes the work of the Redeemer. But this is not in the New Testament the reciprocal mercy between the sinner in need of Redemption and his crucified Redeemer but very one-sidedly and exclusively the work of God's merciful condescension to man. That is why Mt. 5:7 is not proof for the Encyclical's second thesis either, that the Gospel is a synthesis of that "wonderful exchange" of reciprocal mercy between man and the Son of God. Which is why this "wonderful exchange" of reciprocal mercy is not the "easy law of the plan of salvation" either.

The Pope declares, however, using Mt. 5:7 that the "*admirabile commercium*" of reciprocal mercy between man and Christ the Crucified is the "easy law of the plan of salvation," the decisive law of the whole work of Redemption. From the point of view of traditional teaching this is an inexplicable thing to say.

But from the Encyclical's point of view it is quite logical. For in the Pope's theology the sacrifice of the cross is not a redemptive sacrifice in the sense of the New Testament because man is already in a state of grace. Man is *ab origine* in a covenant of grace with God which is substantially identical with the New Covenant of Calvary (cf. 7.5). The Son performs the necessary reparation on the cross due to the faithfulness of the Father to this covenant for the sins of men (cf.

7.1). The sacrifice on the cross is purely an atonement. The ontological reason for this constant faithfulness to the covenant of grace is the Father's giving of Himself to man in the act of Creation in the sense of a substantial union of God with man (cf. *DiM* 7.4 & 5).

On this pantheistic foundation of universal giving of grace that wonderful exchange of mutual mercy receives its specific theological character. The trinitarian foundation for this pantheistic concept is also briefly mentioned in the Encyclical:

– With the third thesis the text moves to a trinitarian statement. This is the thesis: The beatitude of the merciful (Mt. 5:7) does not just reveal "what the human heart is capable of" but at the same time also "the deep mystery of God: that inscrutable unity of Father, Son and Holy Ghost."

No exegete has yet come up with such a trinitarian interpretation of this beatitude from Mt. 5:7. The unity of God cannot consist in the divine Persons showing each other mercy. The English translation of this statement helps towards the confusion. It speaks of "unity." The Latin text, however, says merely "link." If we translate the text more literally the mystery of God reveals

> the inscrutable link between the Father, Son and Holy Ghost in which love which has embraced justice opens the way to mercy which in its turn reveals the perfection of justice (*inscrutabilem Patris et Filii et Spiritus Sancti coniunctionem, in qua amor iustitiam complexus aperit misericordiam viam, quae iustitiae vicissim retegit perfectionem*).

Even with this more accurate translation this part of the Encyclical remains obscure. We can only see that the Pope has brought his conception of justice and mercy into the mystery of the triune God and wants us to know that he understands the mystery of God in the sense of an "economical teaching on the Trinity," so that his ideas of justice and mercy in the acts of the trinitarian God in the history of salvation experience their highest actualisation. In this sense the Pope briefly develops his thoughts concerning the inscrutable mystery of God (cf. *DiM* 8.6).

8.6 The Risen One is the peak of the trinitarian revelation of reciprocal mercy

The trinitarian revelation of reciprocal mercy is performed by the risen Christ. The Pope says (*DiM* 8.6):

> The Paschal Mystery is Christ (*Mysterium proin paschale Christus ipse est*) at the summit of the revelation of the inscrutable mystery of God. It is precisely then that the words pronounced in the Upper Room are completely fulfilled, "He who has seen me has seen the Father" (Jn. 14:9). In fact, Christ, whom the Father "did not spare" (Rom. 8:32) for the sake of man and who in His passion and in the torment of the cross did not obtain human mercy, has revealed in His resurrection the fullness of the love that the Father has for Him and, in Him, for all people. "He is not God of the dead, but of the living" (Mk. 12:27)!

In His resurrection Christ has revealed (*plane*) the God of merciful love, precisely because He accepted the cross as the way to the resurrection. And it is for this reason that—when we recall the cross of Christ, His passion and death—our faith and hope are centred on the Risen One: on that Christ who "on the evening of that day, the first day of the week,...stood among them" in the Upper Room, "where the disciples were,...breathed on them, and said to them: 'Receive the Holy Ghost. Those whose sins you forgive, they are forgiven; those whose sins you retain, they are retained'" (Jn. 20:19-23).

The text should be interpreted in the sense of an economical understanding of the Trinity; of a mutual link (*coniunctio*) of the divine Persons in the merciful plan of salvation.

Thus the Risen One is first the perfect revelation of the *Father's* merciful love for the Son and in Him for all men. It is this love of the Father which is given in like measure from all eternity to the Son and from the beginning of time to man (cf. *DiM* 7.4). It is thus also the same love of the Father which embraces in like measure the Son and humanity. Man is drawn into the trinitarian activity of the divine Persons and the substantial self-giving of the Father because of his nature which by Creation constitutes him as *imago Dei*. With the sentence: The Father is "not a God of the dead, but of the living," *all* men of course are meant for all are "living" *ab origine*.

The Risen One is thus the perfect revelation of the *Son's* merciful love for the Father and *all* men. For the Son "accepted the cross"—which the Father laid upon Him—"as the way to the resurrection" so that the Son could perform reparation for the faithfulness of the Father to His covenant of grace with man for the sins of man.

That is why, when we recall the cross of Christ, His Passion and death, our faith and hope are centred on the risen Son of God who on Easter day reveals the God of mercy through the communication of the *Holy Ghost* and the forgiveness of sins.

In this way the Risen One is the high point of the revelation of the mystery of God because He reveals the merciful love of God in the cooperation of the three divine Persons in the plan of salvation to give reciprocal mercy.

Thus the Pope anchors his main idea in the mystery of the Trinity and justifies it. The texts from Scripture which he quotes are not used in their original sense but are simply used to serve his own way of thinking. Thus the words spoken at the Last Supper, "Who has seen me has seen the Father" are nothing to do with Christ before His Passion but are applied to the Risen Lord. Who sees the Risen One sees the revelation of the faithfulness of the Father to His covenant of grace *ab origine*. He sees in the Risen One the Father as the Redeemer of all men! The communication of the Holy Ghost and the giving of the power to forgive sins do not mean in the context of the Encyclical the giving of priestly power to the disciples and therefore the institution of the sacrament of penance but a general giving of the Holy Ghost and the forgiveness through the Son because He "accepted the cross as the way to the resurrection" as the victim for man's sins.

The Pope's theory of mercy being given to everyone as the "easy law of the plan of salvation" is thus closed.

8.7 The Risen One: the definitive revelation of mercy

With the sentence: the cross of Christ is "a radical revelation of mercy, or rather of the love that goes against what constitutes the very root of evil in the history of man: against sin and death" (*DiM* 8.1) the Pope had begun his consideration on the history of salvation. It finishes with the words (*DiM* 8.7):

> Here is the Son of God (*Ecce Dei Filium*), who in His resurrection experienced in a radical way mercy shown to Himself, that is to say the love of the Father which is more powerful than death. And it is also the same Christ, the Son of God, who at the end of His messianic mission—and, in a certain sense, even beyond the end—reveals Himself as the inexhaustible source of mercy, of the same love that, in a subsequent perspective of the history of salvation in the Church, is to be everlastingly confirmed as more powerful than sin. The Paschal Christ is the definitive incarnation of mercy, its living sign: in the history of salvation and in eschatology. In the same spirit, the liturgy of Eastertide places on our lips the words of the Psalm: *Misericordias Domini in aeternum cantabo* (cf. Ps. 89:2).

The closing answer to the problem of death and sin in the history of man is: Behold the risen Son of God! He reveals the merciful love of the Father which is stronger than death. And: The risen Son of God reveals Himself "as the inexhaustible source of mercy" which will always prove itself in the history of the Church as stronger than sin.

What does this say to the individual who is in danger of death and sin? The answer is:

"The Paschal Christ is the definitive incarnation of mercy, its living sign: in the history of salvation and in eschatology."

Thus merely a "sign"!—because man is saved *ab origine.*

But the resurrection is not just a "sign." It is certainly not a sign of the universal giving of grace but the perfection of Christ's historical work of Redemption whose fruits must be applied to the individual man who is in absolute need of Redemption. Faith is required. In Baptism the Christian is truly united with Christ's death and resurrection. That is why he is dead to sin and snatched from the power of death (cf. Rom 6). In the Risen One eternal life and fellowship with the Blessed Trinity are given to him. The resurrection of the Redeemer is a pledge of his own resurrection of the body to eternal glory at the end of time (I Cor. 15:1ff.).

8.8 Critical review of the main theme of equality and reciprocity in mercy

We can see what is special about the Encyclical's teaching of mercy if we look at traditional teaching:

The conception that the divine Persons are merciful to one another contradicts the very essence of God.

The idea of God's mercy is valid exclusively for the relationship between God and His creatures. Because the distance between Creator and creature is infinite God's mercy towards His creature is an infinite condescension. Any thought of equality and reciprocity must be excluded.

The divine mercy is "the benevolent goodness of God in so far as it removes His creatures' misery especially that of sinners." The passion of compassion which is normally associated with the conception of mercy is not present in God because He is a perfect being but only as the effect of mercy in that He dispels misery (*Summa Theologica* I, Q. 21, a. iii).[39] The idea that a creature could or should show mercy to God is absurd.

In the economy of grace in which man is raised to the participation in the divine nature God's condescension suffers no

[39] Cf. Ludwig Ott, *op. cit.* pp. 57ff.

lessening but rather an increase unto the infinite in divine love. For now it is God Himself who gives Himself to man in grace. God's mercy shows itself at its most generous when after the Fall He sends His Son to perform the Redemption (Lk. 1:78; Jn. 3:16; Tit. 3:4ff.).[40] The idea that the Redemption of sinful man by his divine redeemer is based on equality and reciprocity is quite simply incomprehensible.

Because the Son of God took a human nature in the Incarnation, the God Man can also have the passion of compassion.[41] Jesus weeps at the tomb of Lazarus (Jn. 11:35) and over the city of Jerusalem (Lk. 19:41). The Gospels show insistently the mercy of Christ for all in need especially the contrite sinner (*e.g.,* Lk. 10:30-37; 16:19ff.). Christ's mercy towards the contrite sinner is divine condescension. The idea of equality and reciprocity is unthinkable.

Jesus, because of His human nature, could also in His human life receive mercy. He neither called for man's mercy in His Passion, the work of Redemption nor did He want or expect deliverance from the hand of His enemies. But He did receive some human mercy even on the cross (cf. *DiM* 7.2 where it says the opposite). For His mother, His beloved disciple and the holy women (Jn. 19:25ff.) were also standing at the cross. This human compassionate mercy is, however, not a constitutive part of the work of Redemption, it is not the "easy law of the plan of salvation."

We must distinguish between God's mercy and man's mercy. But even human mercy is not based on the principle of equality and reciprocity. It is a form of charity which turns to the person in need for God's sake.[42] The conception implies the bending down of someone stronger to a fellow human being in need without any expectation of a merciful repayment which

---

40 *Ibid.*

41 *Ibid.*

42 Hieronymus Noldin, *Summa Theologiae moralis* (Heidelberg 1944, Editio 28), II, pp. 90ff.—Joseph Mausbach/Gustav Ermecke, *Katholische Moraltheologie* [*Catholic Moral Theology*] (Münster 1959, 11th edition), II, pp. 147ff.

at any rate generally cannot be given (cf. Lk. 10:25ff.). It is certain that the Christian can trust in the beatitude of the merciful and can expect to be rewarded for his works of mercy by the mercy of God.

The principle of equality and the common experience of reciprocity in mercy which runs through the whole plan of salvation in the Encyclical and therefore also through the relationship between God and man is only to be understood from the background of a pantheistic theory of a universal giving of grace. It is the logical consequence of the idea already mooted by Cardinal Wojtyla that love is only possible between equals.[43]

9. The Mother of mercy

In Karl Lehmann's commentary this article is introduced thus, "The Pope brings all the threads of his theological design together into a brief sketch 'The Mother of mercy'."[44] This sketch is, however, not just the convergence of all the theological ideas that the Pope has put forward in his Encyclical but also the concentration on the central idea of the reciprocity of mercy. It is also, apart from its length, a good example of the Pope's poetic style regarding his command of Sacred Scripture and the way he thinks theologically.

9.1 The new Marian vision of mercy in the history of salvation

The previous article (8) ends with the verse from the psalm "I will sing the mercies of the Lord for ever" (Ps. 89:2). The Pope takes up this verse and continues (*DiM* 9.1):

> These words of the Church at Easter reecho in the fullness of their prophetic content the words that Mary uttered dur-

[43] Karol Wojtyla, *Liebe und Verantwortung* [*Love and Responsibility*] (Munich 1979).

[44] [*Threatened Man and the Power of Mercy.* Pope John Paul's Encyclical on God's mercy] (Freiburg i. Br. 1981), p. 105.

> ing her visit to Elizabeth, the wife of Zechariah,
>
> "His mercy is...from generation to generation" (Lk. 1:50). At the very moment of the Incarnation, these words open up a new perspective of the history of salvation. After the resurrection of Christ, this perspective is new on both the historical and the eschatological level. From that time onwards there is a succession of new generations of individuals in the immense human family, in ever-increasing dimensions; there is also a succession of new generations of the People of God, marked with the Sign of the Cross and of the resurrection and "sealed" (cf. II Cor. 1:21ff.) with the sign of the Paschal Mystery of Christ, the absolute revelation of the mercy that Mary proclaimed on the threshold of her kinswoman's house, "His mercy is...from generation to generation" (Lk. 1:50).

The verse from the *Magnificat*, "His mercy is from generation to generation to them that fear him" (Lk. 1:50) is as it were the framework and main idea from the beginning (*DiM* 5.1) to the end (*DiM* 9.1) of the New Testament section of the Encyclical. But in the Encyclical's version, half the quotation is missing. The condition is missing, God's mercy is "to them that fear Him." It is in this typical abbreviation that Mary's words form the biblical foundation of the Pope's abbreviated "Mariology."

That is why God's mercy in the Pope's new vision of the history of salvation embraces all generations of the family of man and thereby the People of God. The generations of the People of God are marked with the Sign and "sealed" with the sign of the Paschal Mystery of Christ but that only means that they are in possession of the "absolute revelation of the mercy" (*consummatae revelationis istius misericordiae*) which embraces the whole of humanity with no exceptions *ab origine* in the covenant of grace. The human race is the invisible Church! This view is "a fruit of the Council" (cf. *DiM* 1.4) and the ever repeated teaching of the Pope.[45] This is the new part of

[45] Karol Wojtyla, *Sign of Contradiction*, pp. 37-39;—Cf. Part I, pp. 48-78; Part II/1, pp. 65-86.

the "new (Marian) vision of the plan of salvation" of mercy.

Mary's words, "His mercy is from generation to generation" proclaim—as does the Paschal Mystery—divine mercy in the sense of a universal giving of grace!

9.2 Mary's part in the revelation of the universal giving of grace

Mary, by her words concerning God's mercy, has not only opened and declared (*pandere*) a new vision of the plan of salvation of mercy but also in a unique way has a part in the revelation of divine mercy. The Pope goes on (*DiM* 9.2):

> Mary is also the one who obtained mercy in a particular and exceptional way, as no other person has. At the same time, still in an exceptional way, she made possible with the sacrifice of her heart her own participation in revealing God's mercy. This sacrifice is intimately linked with the cross of her Son, at the foot of which she was to stand on Calvary. Her sacrifice is a unique sharing in the revelation of mercy, that is, a sharing in the absolute fidelity of God to His own love, to the covenant that He willed from eternity and that He entered into in time with man, with the people, with humanity; it is a sharing in that revelation that was definitively fulfilled through the cross. *No one has experienced, to the same degree as the Mother of the Crucified One*, the mystery of the cross, the overwhelming encounter of divine transcendent justice with love: that "kiss" given by mercy to justice (Ps. 85:11). No one has received into his heart, as much as Mary did, that mystery, that truly divine dimension of the Redemption effected on Calvary by means of the death of the Son, together with the sacrifice of her maternal heart, together with her definitive "*fiat.*"

Thus the Pope also reads his main idea of the reciprocity of mercy into Mary's *Magnificat*. Mary knows what she is talking about: She has experienced mercy like no other and she has given mercy through the sacrifice of her maternal heart like no other. That is why she personally has a part in the revelation of divine mercy.

The God of this mercy as has been emphasised is the God of the indissoluble covenant of grace with man *ab origine*. Mary's sharing in this revelation of divine mercy means the communication of the universal giving of grace! "No one has received into his heart, as much as Mary did, that mystery": She is the co-revealer of the universal giving of grace!

9.3 Mary's part in the decree of the Trinity

Because no one has experienced the mystery of the cross like the mother of the Crucified One and co-operated with it by the sacrifice of her maternal heart,

"Mary, then" continues the Pope (*DiM* 9.3),

> is the one who *has the deepest knowledge of the mystery of God's mercy*. She knows its price, she knows how great it is. In this sense, we call her the *Mother of mercy*: our Lady of mercy, or Mother of divine mercy; in each one of these titles there is a deep theological meaning, for they express the special preparation of her soul, of her whole personality, so that she was able to perceive, through the complex events, first of Israel, then of every individual and of the whole of humanity, that mercy of which "from generation to generation" (Lk. 1:50) people become sharers according to the eternal design of the most Holy Trinity.

According to the text Mary, because of the participation in the design of the Blessed Trinity which was given to her, possessed the capability of knowing (*dispicere*) in the history of man the universal giving of grace of God's mercy "from generation to generation."

The knowledge of universal salvation is said to come to Mary directly from the design of the trinitarian God.—All this the Pope gets from half a verse of the *Magnificat*.

9.4 Mary's participation in the messianic mission of her Son

Mary does not just have a unique part in the revelation of her Son but also in His messianic mission (*DiM* 9.4):

> The above titles which we attribute to the Mother of God speak of her principally, however, as the Mother of the Crucified and Risen One; as the One who, having obtained mercy in an exceptional way, in an equally exceptional way "merits" that mercy throughout her earthly life and, particularly, at the foot of the cross of her Son; and finally as the one who, through her hidden and at the same time incomparable sharing in the messianic mission of her Son, was called in a special way to bring close to people that love which He had come to reveal: the love that finds its most concrete expression *vis-à-vis* the suffering, the poor, those deprived of their own freedom, the blind, the oppressed and sinners, just as Christ spoke of them in the words of the prophecy of Isaiah, first in the synagogue at Nazareth (cf. Lk. 4:18) and then in response to the question of the messengers of John the Baptist (cf. Lk. 7:22).

The easy law of reciprocal mercy runs through the whole of Mary's life. The messianic programme of Christ and the Church is also Mary's programme. This programme has already been analysed in some detail (cf. *DiM* 3.8).

9.5 The maternal revelation of divine mercy

What is special about Mary's participation in the announcement of the messianic revelation of mercy is dealt with by the Encyclical in the following way (*DiM* 9.5):

> It was precisely this "merciful" love, which is manifested above all in contact with moral and physical evil, that the heart of her who was the Mother of the Crucified and Risen One shared in singularly and exceptionally—that Mary shared in. In her and through her, this love continues to be revealed

> in the history of the Church and of humanity. This revelation is especially fruitful because in the Mother of God it is based upon the unique tact of her maternal heart, on her particular sensitivity, on her particular fitness to reach all those who most easily accept the merciful love of a mother. This is one of the great life-giving mysteries of Christianity, a mystery intimately connected with the mystery of the Incarnation.

Not only in Christ but also in the mother of Christ God's mercy is revealed in the history of the Church and humanity. In the mother of Christ the revelation of divine mercy is brought closer to man in a motherly way. There is, therefore in Mary a motherly revelation of the God who is full of mercy.

This motherly revelation is similarly based on the law of the reciprocity of mercy and the universal giving of grace *ab origine*.

9.6 The motherhood of Mary in the economy of grace

The pious Marian considerations in the Encyclical end with a long quotation from *Gaudium et Spes* (62) whose basic content summed up is (*DiM* 9.6):

The motherhood of Mary in the order of grace lasts without interruption from the *Fiat* of the Annunciation to the end of the pilgrimage of the brethren of her son.

The new Marian vision of the Pope's history of salvation is based on Mary's words, "His mercy is from generation to generation." But this is only half of Mary's words of praise. The whole verse reads:

> And his mercy is from generation unto generations, to them that fear him (Lk. 1:50).

The Encyclical which elsewhere does quote the full verse (*e.g., DiM* 5.1) suppresses however the decisive condition in this fundamental presentation of the Mother of divine mercy. His mercy is for "them that fear him." This condition in the biblical text contradicts a general giving of divine mercy simply to all and sundry, it contradicts the Encyclical's theory of the universal giving of grace. The complete verse of the *Magnificat* (Lk. 1:50) takes away the biblical foundation of the Pope's vision of the history of salvation.

CHAPTER VI

A Picture of our Generation*

As he did in *Redemptor Hominis*, following the basic theological part of *Dives in Misericordia*, the Pope gives a picture of our generation (*DiM* 10-12) to whom his Gospel of mercy is directed (*DiM* 13-15).

This picture is taken from the pastoral constitution *Gaudium et Spes* and is necessarily only a sketch. Because the theme of our study is the Pope's theology we limit ourselves to a brief look at the main ideas contained in the last few chapters of the Encyclical, quoting the more important texts and a few extra remarks.

10. The generation of the historical change**

The theological framework in which the Pope considers our generation is divine mercy (*DiM* 10.1):

> We have every right to believe that our generation too was included in the words of the Mother of God when she glorified that mercy shared in "from generation to generation" by those who allow themselves to be guided by the fear of God.

This time the Pope quotes the whole of the verse from the *Magnificat* without, however, drawing the logical conclusions from it (cf. *DiM* 9).

The first point of reference for our generation to be named

---

* The chapter title in the English translation is "Mercy...from Generation to Generation."

** The article title in the English translation is, "An Image of Our Generation."

is the most general (*DiM* 10.1):

> In fact, all of us now living on earth are the generation that is aware of the approach of the third millennium and that profoundly feels the change that is occurring in history.

The approach of the third millennium holds a significant place in the Pope's conception of the history of salvation (cf. *RH* 1.1-2).[1]

The Encyclical first mentions the privileges then the difficulties which mark our generation:

This present generation is privileged by the great advances "in the field of science and technology and in that of social and cultural life." Thereby man "has acquired deeper knowledge of the laws of social behaviour."

The general progress has also marked modern man's consciousness (*DiM* 10.2):

> He has seen the obstacles and distances between individuals and nations dissolve or shrink through an increased sense of what is universal, through a clearer awareness of the unity of the human race, through the acceptance of mutual dependence in authentic solidarity, and through the desire and possibility of making contact with one's brothers and sisters beyond artificial geographic divisions and national or racial limits.

The most obvious sign of the mentality of our generation is thus the clear consciousness of the unity of the human family and of a general brotherhood of man which goes beyond any "artificial borders."

The Pope considers the historical development from the point of view of "progress" which has been achieved by the growing exchange of material, intellectual and cultural riches of the various peoples.

But precisely this "great progress" brings also great difficul-

---

[1] Cf. Part II/1, pp. 49-61.

ties with it.

The main difficulty he sees in the fact that this progress at the moment is still very often the "privilege of the industrialised nations." But he does not deny (*DiM* 10.2):

> that the prospect of enabling every people and every country to benefit from it has long ceased to be a mere utopia when there is a real political desire for it.

The Pope sees "progress" as a process of growth with immanent difficulties "which is the same for all growth." It is a question of "The picture of the world today also containing shadows and imbalances."

The pastoral constitution *Gaudium et Spes* (10) has discovered the deeper context: it sees these imbalances in the context of every "imbalance" which "lies in the heart of man." Man feels on the one hand his created shortcomings and on the other the longing for a higher life to which he is called (*DiM* 10.3):

> "And so he feels himself divided, and the result is a host of discords in social life" (*GS* 10).

The Pope sees a growing number who in the present development of the world "are asking the most fundamental of all questions" about man's being and the meaning of life (cf. *DiM* 10.4). But the "tensions and threats" in the world have become more manifest since the Second Vatican Council (cf. *DiM* 10.5).

Here are a few remarks about how the Encyclical sees the world:

The general striving after "One World" has already been influencing consciousness and also contemporary politics long before the Second Vatican Council. That is why the highest Magisterium, Catholic social teaching and moral theology have already taken this into account. The Catholic way of looking at it may be seen in the classical theology textbook from

Mausbach-Ermecke,

> The tendency to legally organise men and their organisations of united peoples in states even as far a making a world state organisation is growing every day stronger due to the growing national and international interdependence in all social areas. The Church does not just take note of this but supports it.

At the same time it accepts the fact of the unity of the family of man in which all men are brothers and sisters by nature and because of their calling to grace and as such should live together and as people and states have the right to their own culture and independence. The universal community of the family of man is once again ordered towards the new universal family of the children of God in Christ, the Church. Thus Christ is "the principle of life of human society" (Pius XII) through His Church. Because Christ is the love of God made man such an order proceeds from love.[2]

The unity of man in true solidarity and universal brotherhood in a "world State" beyond all "artificial borders" like race, nation and religion is, however, the declared aim of the liberal-enlightened, Freemasonic efforts.[3] These ideas and not what the Church believes mark the consciousness of our generation. The Pope describes the general striving after unity with the usual categories of progress and thus draws a realistic picture of the spiritual profile of our age.

At important points, however, clearly defined borders and critical objections from the classical teaching of the Church are missing. It should be clearly said that quite successful "one World" efforts of a political and socialist and liberal internationalism uproot man culturally and thereby destroy him. Man is by nature a cultural creature.[4] Man as a brother or sister

---

[2] Cf. Joseph Mausbach/Gustav Ermecke, *Katholische Moraltheologie* (Münster/Westf. 1961), III, pp. 136ff.

[3] Cf. Johannes Tothdranz, *Die kommende "Diktatur der Humanität"* [*The Coming Dictatorship of Humanity*] (Durach 1990), Vol. I-III.

[4] Johannes Dörmann, *Die Eine Kirche in allen Kulturen—Das Problem*

"beyond artificial geographic divisions and national or racial limits" *(ultra arte factas partitiones geographicas vel fines nationum aut stirpium*) is an abstract idea and so the presuppositions for the desired unity remain a similarly abstract and rootless humanity which is controlled by a world democracy just as abstract and lacking in any history.

The expansion of scientific and technical developments of western civilisation throughout the world cannot be understood adequately with evolutionist categories of progress nor simply declared a "privilege of the industrialised countries" which could be enjoyed by all countries as long as a real political desire for it existed.

The problem "in all these developments" are by no means just "difficulties" or "imbalances" which are a symptom "of all growth" and in the end seated in "man's heart" (cf. *DiM* 10.3). Rather the reality is a global cultural change which is destroying whole races, peoples and cultures in their spiritual and religious foundations. One of the main causes is the decline in culture brought about by modern science and civilisation in the rest of the world. From this cultural decay comes necessarily a global change in culture which is above every individual and causes crises of whole continents.[5]

The question is, will embracing the modern world which is ruled by the spirit of the Enlightenment open the way for it to becoming Christian?

---

der Indigenisation [*The One Church in All Cultures—The Problem of Inculturation*]. In: *Weisheit Gottes—Weisheit der Welt. Festschrift für Joseph Kardinal Ratzinger* [*God's Wisdom—the World's Wisdom. A Testimonial for Joseph Cardinal Ratzinger*] (60), (St. Ottilien 1987), II, pp. 1039-1058.

5 Johannes Dörmann, *Die Eine Kirche und die vielen Kulturen* [*The One Church and the many cultures*]. In: Josef Schreiner (pub.), *Die Kirche im Wandel der Gesellschaft* [*The Church in a Changing Society*] (Würzburg 1970), pp. 240-257.—The series of articles: *Die Eine Kirche in allen Völkern und Kulturen* [*The One Church in All Nations and Cultures*] I-XII. In: *Pastoralblatt für die Diözesen Aachen, Berlin, etc.* [*Diocesan newsletter for Aachen, Berlin etc.*] 8 (1985) and *Theologisches* 4 (1985)-8 (1985).

11. Sources of uneasiness

For the Pope "existential fear" is a further sign of our present generation. Even in modern philosophy and psychology "fear" is a basic component of human existence.[6] The Pope says "existential fear" is empirically caused and nourished by a feeling of being under threat. He refers to his Encyclical *Redemptor Hominis* which has already mentioned this threat (*RH* 15-17). He therefore summarises:

Man's increasing feeling of being under threat is born of the stockpiling of nuclear weapons, of the consequences of a materialist civilisation which "places things above persons," of the means invented by this type of society making it easier to fall victim to the abuse of power by others. Finally he says (*DiM* 11.2):

> Man rightly fears falling victim to an oppression that will deprive him of his interior freedom, of the possibility of expressing the truth of which he is convinced, of the faith that he professes, of the ability to obey the voice of conscience that tells him the right path to follow.

This point of view is stressed once more: for greater than the threat to physical life is the threat to (*DiM* 11.3): "what is essentially human, what is intimately bound up with the dignity of the person and his or her right to truth and freedom."

Thus the Encyclical comes to the sensitive heart of man's existentially being threatened. This is the threat to the dignity of the person with his right to freedom of conscience and religion (cf. also *DiM* 11.5).

To the threats from without come the reproaches from within: For the threats from without take place "against a background of gigantic remorse." The cause of this is that in the "various socio-economic systems" of the human family there is consumerism and pleasure on the one hand and misery and

---

[6] See H. Rombach and J.B. Metz, article *Angst*, in *LThK*, I, col. 556-559.

hunger on the other. Thus the North-South divide is addressed. Concerning this the Pope's worried commentary says, the "contemporary economics and materialistic civilisation" which is built on very shaky foundations "does not allow the human family to break free from such radically unjust situations" (*DiM* 11.4).

This generalising moral verdict on "contemporary economics" and the demand for a new world economic order[7] contained in it could, in that it gives no concrete suggestions to remedy the situation, sound rather moralising and unwittingly open the door to revolutionary ideas.[8]

This picture of the modern world in which there is so much physical and moral suffering and in which "at the same time human freedom, conscience and religion" are also threatened explains "the uneasiness felt by contemporary man" (*DiM* 11.5).

The Pope does not stop at describing this uneasiness. He also inquires into the causes and shows the way for the future: Although there is no lack of people who have discovered the causes of this uneasiness and fought against it using technology, wealth and power, the uneasiness in the heart of man is not quelled by these measures. This uneasiness, as the Second Vatican Council says, concerns (*DiM* 11.5):

> the fundamental problems of all human existence. It is linked with the very sense of man's existence in the world, and is an uneasiness for the future of man and all humanity; it demands decisive solutions, which now seem to be forcing themselves upon the human race.

---

7 In more detail *Redemptor Hominis* 16. See Part II/1, pp. 196-203.

8 Franz Josef Micha, *Hilfe für Entwicklungsländer—ein Problem.* [*Help for the Developing Lands—a Problem*]. In: *Politisch-Soziale Korrespondenz* [*Social Political Correspondence*] [= *PSK*] 8 (Bonn 1959), No. 3, pp. 8-11.—Johannes Dörmann, *Politische Aspekte der Entwicklungshilfe* [*Political Aspects of Development Aid*]. In: *PSK* 8 (1959), No. 5, pp. 7-10. Also, *Vorschläge zum Problem der Entwicklungshilfe.* In: *PSK* 8 (1959), No. 9, pp. 7-11.

So far the Pope has concentrated on two things: the threat to freedom of opinion, conscience and religion which is closely linked to "the dignity of the person and his right to truth and freedom" and the "inequality amongst people and nations."

If we join to these demands for freedom and equality the demand made already in the previous article for universal brotherhood in one humanity (cf. *DiM* 10.2) then the spiritual profile which the Encyclical draws of the driving forces of our contemporary world become clear: The unity of humanity in liberty, equality and fraternity beyond all "artificial borders."

Thus the Pope has drawn a picture of the main characteristics of the general consciousness which incontrovertibly marks the present generation in western civilisation and which are being spread over the whole world by the modern means of communication and international politics. However, he does not just describe the spiritual and political profile but uses the jargon of modern history of freedom and integrates it significantly into his own concept.

The Encyclical broadens its scope by asking about the "ethical character" of the problems at the root of all tensions.

12. The ethical character of the tensions and struggles*

The new found sense of justice in the modern world is another important sign for the Pope of the consciousness of the modern generation.

The Church's teaching has obviously contributed much to a sense of social justice. But it can hardly be disputed that the "sense of justice which has been reawakened in the modern world" comes mainly from the spirit "of this world" and bears the marks of revolutionary *égalité*, socialism and liberalism on its forehead.

How does the Encyclical describe the newly awakened sense of justice?

---

* Title of article in English translation, "Is Justice Enough?"

It highlights the fact that the "modern world's sense of justice" emphasises that which goes against justice in relationships between individuals, social groups and "classes," between individual peoples and states. Thus begins the Pope's ethical consideration (*DiM* 12.1):

> This deep and varied trend, at the basis of which the contemporary human conscience has placed justice, gives proof of the ethical character of the tensions and struggles pervading the world.

Justice is the universal category in which the Encyclical understands and considers the ethical character of the worldwide tensions and struggles.

The Pope welcomes unreservedly the reawakening of the consciousness for justice in the modern world and at the same time points out that the Church shares with man the burning desire for a just life in every area and gives thought to the various aspects of justice herself. The proof of this is Catholic social teaching according to whose principles proceed the education and formation of human consciences in the spirit of justice (*DiM* 12.2). The Pope is therefore considering "social justice" without, however, using this term.

One expects the Encyclical to present the reawakened sense of justice in some concrete way, to show its historical sources and to criticise the systems of communism, socialism and liberalism where they disagree with Catholic social teaching. But that does not happen, rather the Pope goes his own way, following his own aims.

He criticises social reality in a general way. We cannot after all overlook the fact that these programmes which started off with justice have often gone other ways in practise. Although justice was always quoted it was the negative forces which somehow got the upper hand and decided what was done. This contradicts the very meaning of justice (*DiM* 12.3):

> which by its nature tends to establish equality and harmony

between the parties in conflict.

Thus the Pope defines the essence of justice. Thence he goes to Sacred Scripture to show immediately the boundaries of his definition (*DiM* 12.3): Christ challenged the Jews who were faithful to the law which was expressed by the phrase, "Eye for an eye, tooth for a tooth" (Mt. 5:38). This form of justice which in those days had already distorted the true notion is the present day model. From this the Pope says (*DiM* 12.3):

> The experience of the past and of our own time demonstrates that justice alone is not enough, that it can lead to the negation and destruction of itself, if that deeper power, which is love, is not allowed to shape human life in its various dimensions.

Thus the Pope's definition of justice becomes clearer: the word's root meaning aims at "equality and harmony between the parties in conflict." Justice in the bitter style of "an eye for an eye" needs complementing with love in man's living together. This aspect does not detract from justice but just shows the necessity of "drawing from the powers of the spirit which condition the very order of justice, powers which are still more profound" (*DiM* 12.3).

Whether the additional characterisation of justice as "eye for an eye, tooth for a tooth" really defines the content of what justice was then and is now or not remains unclear. The Pope develops a more precise definition of justice later on (*DiM* 14). Here what is important to him is saying that justice must be complemented by love.

Simply to say that justice is at the root of all tensions and struggles in our day is obviously not enough. Therefore the Pope in a sort of appendix completes his picture of our generation with a list of other ethical deficiencies (*DiM* 12.5):

> Moreover, one cannot fail to be worried by the decline of

> many fundamental values, which constitute an unquestionable good not only for Christian morality but simply for human morality, for moral culture: these values include respect for human life from the moment of conception, respect for marriage in its indissoluble unity, and respect for the stability of the family. Moral permissiveness strikes especially at this most sensitive sphere of life and society. Hand in hand with this go the crisis of truth in human relationships, lack of responsibility for what one says, the purely utilitarian relationship between individual and individual, the loss of a sense of the authentic common good and the ease with which this good is alienated. Finally, there is the "desacralisation" that often turns into "dehumanisation": the individual and the society for whom nothing is "sacred" suffer moral decay, in spite of appearances.

It is amazing how the Pope presents fundamental Christian values "simply" and "unquestionably" as "human morality" and "moral culture," when it is obvious that the varying forms of morality are conditioned by the different religions and philosophies and that, for example, the indissolubility of marriage in no way belongs to a general "moral culture" of man. This is specific to the Catholic sacrament of marriage.

It is equally amazing that the Pope only looks at the ethical character and does not consider the religious character of the tensions and struggles throughout the world based on the consciousness of our generation. Does religion play no significant rôle in our generation and is, therefore, the declaration of freedom of religion the solution to these tensions?

The religious character of the tensions in the consciousness of our generation would make us consider the religious situation of peoples and cultures and therefore the New Testament view of the world and history. From the point of view of the New Testament religious tensions are the most important. The "world," since and because of Christ, is in a state of crisis. In Christ God has already given His judgment on the world. Even in the modern world it is a question of belief or unbelief, of man's eternal salvation or damnation. This diacritic mission of Christ and His disciples is continued by the Church in a great historical "judgment" (cf. Jn. 16:7ff.). The proclamation of the Kingdom of God is the beginning of the divine crisis in the history of man. It is the character and mission of the Church in the history of salvation to cause this crisis. In this sense the Church is and remains a constant source of crisis in the world.

Viewed from the mission of the Church we get the points of view for the evangelisation of peoples and cultures, for the problems of a world-wide culture change, for conflicts with the spiritual values of the modern world and its slogans of "liberty, equality and fraternity."[9]—Has the salt lost its savour?

[9] Cf. Johannes Dörmann, [*The One Church and the Many Cultures*]. In: Josef Schreiner (pub.), [*The Church in a Changing Society*] (Würzburg 1970), pp. 140-257.—Johannes Dörmann, *Metamorphose der griechisch-römischen Kultur durch das Evangelium.* [*Metamorphosis of Graeco-Roman Culture by the Gospel*] In: *Begegnung der Kulturen in Ost und West. Festschrift für Hyogmyon Kwon* [*Meeting of Cultures in East and West. Testimonial for Hyogmyon Kwon*] (60). (1967), pp. 109-131.—Christian Gnilka, *Chrêsis. Die Methode der Kirchenväter im Umgang mit der antiken Kultur* [*The Method of the Fathers of the Church in the Context of Ancient Cultures*], Vols. I & II (Basel 1984; 1993).

CHAPTER VII

GOD'S MERCY IN THE CHURCH'S MISSION

In the last part of the Encyclical (*DiM* 13-15) the Pope gives a brief sketch of what he intends to say (*DiM* VII). The theme is to be:

> In connection with this picture of our generation (= *DiM* VI), a picture which cannot fail to cause profound anxiety, there come to mind once more those words which, by reason of the Incarnation of the Son of God, resounded in Mary's *Magnificat*, and which sing of "mercy from generation to generation." The Church of our time, constantly pondering the eloquence of these inspired words, and applying them to the sufferings of the great human family, must become more particularly and profoundly conscious of the need to bear witness in her whole mission to God's mercy, following in the footsteps of the tradition of the Old and New Covenant, and above all of Jesus Christ Himself and His Apostles.

The Pope once again begins with Mary's *Magnificat* "by reason of the Incarnation." Once again he only quotes half of the verse—deliberately—and thereby shows already how he understands the mercy of God. Since, according to his teaching, the Son of God formally united Himself with the whole of humanity in the Incarnation (cf. *RH* 13; 14) God's mercy also embraces the whole of humanity, our generation included, with no conditions. The "inspired words" of Mary which "the Church ponders in her heart" announce thus the new teaching of the universal giving of grace (cf. *DiM* 1.4).

The Pope's call to the Church seems to contradict this when he asks her to become "more profoundly conscious" of her mission from the sources of revelation and tradition. But the new understanding of her mission is not to be found in these sources.

This is how the Encyclical is set out in its last section:

> The Church must bear witness to the mercy of God revealed in Christ, in the whole of His mission as Messiah, professing it in the first place as a salvific truth of faith and as necessary for a life in harmony with faith, and then seeking to introduce it and to make it incarnate in the lives both of her faithful and as far as possible in the lives of all people of good will. Finally, the Church—professing mercy and remaining always faithful to it—has the right and the duty to call upon the mercy of God, imploring it in the face of all the manifestations of physical and moral evil, before all the threats that cloud the whole horizon of the life of humanity today.

The Encyclical, therefore, considers the Church's mission in the world, which is threatened from all sides, in a threefold way: The Church must profess the truth of God's mercy in agreement with Christ's messianic mission and the faith (*DiM* 13), she must try to realise this in the lives of the faithful and of all men (*DiM* 14) and she must call upon the mercy of God in prayer for the whole of humanity (*DiM* 15).

13. The Church professes and proclaims God's mercy

In his introductory words the Pope has emphasised that his teaching on mercy agrees with revelation and the whole of tradition. Thus he now begins with the fundamental statement (*DiM* 13.1):

> The Church must profess and proclaim God's mercy in all its truth, as it has been handed down to us by revelation. We have sought, in the foregoing pages of the present document, to give at least an outline of this truth, which finds such rich expression in the whole of Sacred Scripture and in Sacred Tradition.

The text suggests to the reader that the truth contained in Sacred Scripture and Tradition is identical with that contained in the Encyclical and is faithfully reproduced "in this document." The truth is that this is not the case. Rather it is obvious that the whole of revelation and tradition undergo a fundamental reinterpretation by the theological principles of "this document." The Pope hijacks Scripture and tradition for his own completely new ideas.

Therefore it is not the authentic but a reinterpreted revelation of divine mercy which the Encyclical says is the contents of the Church's mission and which the Pope gives to the Church as the truth of Sacred Scripture and Tradition in the following articles (*DiM* 13-15). This takes place according to the general principle: *accommodata renovatio Ecclesiae ad intra et ad extra*: the new teaching is brought into the Church's Faith in order to make it agree with the teaching of the Second Vatican Council.[1]

The Pope begins with a general view of the various areas of Church life (*DiM* 13.1-3): The Church takes the truth about mercy which is contained in the Encyclical and puts them in the readings of the Liturgy and expresses them in the various forms of personal and communal piety (*DiM* 13.1). The Church professes and lives this truth of God's mercy "by constantly contemplating Christ, concentrating on Him, on His life and on His Gospel, on His cross and resurrection, on His whole mystery" by looking on Him who said, "Who has seen me has seen the Father" (*DiM* 13.2). The Church is living authentically "when she brings people close to the sources of the Saviour's mercy, of which she is the trustee and dispenser." She herself approaches these sources of mercy by constantly meditating on the word of God, by celebrating the Eucharist and the sacrament of Penance or Reconciliation (*DiM* 13.3).

That could also be understood in the traditional sense. The generality of the statement means it could be understood in

---

[1] For the *accommodata renovatio* see in more detail Part I pp. 15-46.

any way. But there can be no doubt in which sense this document's pious representation of the Church's faith and life is to be understood. The ambiguous character of the text can be seen in a more detailed analysis of the following paragraphs (*DiM* 13.4-8) in which the Pope goes into more detail. He speaks more about the Sacrament of Reconciliation by applying the theological principles of this document to the inner process of penance. In his own words (*DiM* 13.4):

> It is precisely because sin exists in the world, which "God so loved...that he gave his only Son," (Jn. 3:16) that God, who "is love," (I Jn. 4:8) cannot reveal Himself otherwise than as mercy. This corresponds not only to the most profound truth of that love which God is, but also to the whole interior truth of man and of the world which is man's temporary homeland.

No, God does not have to, He can do otherwise! Only if God clings to His indissoluble covenant of grace with man *ab origine* ***must*** He reveal Himself as mercy ***because*** there is sin in the world. Only with the presupposition that man is created out of the same love which the Father has for His crucified Son as the inviolable image and likeness of God (cf. *DiM* 7.4) is the sacrifice of the cross a necessary satisfaction which the Son must perform for the faithfulness of the Father to His fatherhood for the sins of men. Then this mercy is representative of the deepest truth of God in His constant faithfulness to Himself and to His covenant of mercy. Then this mercy is representative of the inner truth of man's dignity of being a son which he cannot lose.

The Encyclical's thesis which joins sin in the world to God's love even unto the giving up of His Son and therefore produces this ***must*** of mercy is simply the logical consequence of the axiom of the universal giving of grace *ab origine.*

From the point of view of the Church's teaching on the Redemption we must say this about the quoted text: Just as God was absolutely free from any exterior force or inner obligation to create the world,[2] so He was also not obliged to redeem it.[3] Just as God's goodness did not necessitate the Creation,[4] so God's love did not necessitate the Redemption.[5] For "the Redemption is a completely free act of divine love and divine mercy (*libertas contradictionis*). If the raising of man to the state of the supernatural order is a free gift of divine love then even more so the restoration of the supernatural covenant of life with God which was destroyed by mortal sin."[6] The Incarnation and the sacrifice of the cross are the absolutely free response of God's love to man's sin.

Even with the presupposition of God's free decision to give supernatural grace, the Incarnation was not absolutely necessary after the commission of sin. St. Anselm of Canterbury teaches: If God decided from all eternity in spite of Him foreseeing Original Sin to create man and give him sanctifying grace then it was also due to a freely taken decision that the necessity of redeeming man after sin was committed came about (*necessitas consequens*).[7] This did not, however, need to be the Incarnation and the sacrifice of the cross.[8]

St. Thomas teaches, with St. Augustine, "that God due to His omnipotence could have redeemed man by many other means (*libertas specificationis*) (*Summa Theologica* III, Q. 1, a. ii). It would be making God's omnipotence, wisdom and mercy less if we thought the Incarnation was the only way in which God could have redeemed man. Without going against justice God can give pardon and grace to the penitent sinner without any satisfaction or with inadequate satisfaction." Only if we presupposed that "God required an adequate satisfaction would the Incarnation have been necessary" (hypothetic

2 Ludwig Ott, *Fundamentals of Catholic Dogma*, p. 81.

3 *Ibid.* p. 176-177.

4 *Ibid.* p. 81.

5 *Ibid.* p. 176-177.

6 *Ibid.*

7 *Ibid.* p. 177.

8 *Ibid.* p. 176ff.

necessity).[9]

The question is, can the Encyclical's thesis be interpreted in the sense of a hypothetic necessity?

The problem is as follows: If the Father created man as His inviolable image and likeness out of the same love which He has for His crucified Son then He cannot reveal His love for man in any other way than by giving His Son up when sin is committed. If the Father is joined to His adoptive sons (cf. *DiM* 7.4 & 5) by an indissoluble ontological bond because of His giving Himself to man then He cannot do otherwise than reveal Himself as mercy given that sin is in the world. The reasoning is in itself watertight but the premises contradict authentic revelation.

The Pope's thesis implies an infinite love of God for man with no conditions attached, a mercy that is infinite and with no boundaries. That is precisely what the following text explains (*DiM* 13.5):

> Mercy in itself, as a perfection of the infinite God, is also infinite. Also infinite therefore and inexhaustible is the Father's readiness to receive the prodigal children who return to His home. Infinite are the readiness and power of forgiveness which flow continually from the marvellous value of the sacrifice of the Son. No human sin can prevail over this power or even limit it. On the part of man only a lack of good will can limit it, a lack of readiness to be converted and to repent, in other words, persistence in obstinacy, opposing grace and truth, especially in the face of the witness of the cross and resurrection of Christ.

The text seems to reproduce the message of the Gospel at first sight. Unconditioned trust in the mercy of the Father and in the sacrifice of the Son is a Christian's firm belief. For the Redeemer came to save what was lost. That is why the greatest sinner, if he does penance, is received by the Father with the

---

9 *Ibid.*

joy of the Gospel just like the Prodigal Son.

But the text must be understood from the Encyclical's premises. That is why we must remember: As the necessity of the Redemption does not follow necessarily from the perfect love of God (see above) so the unconditioned infiniteness of His mercy does not follow from the perfection of the infinite God. There is no real Prodigal Son in the Encyclical for there he never really lost his (supernatural) dignity of being a son (*DiM* 6.2 & 3) because "this basic value of man can never be destroyed" (cf. *DiM* 14.12). That is why—in spite of the impressive formulation—the "infinite mercy of God" in the Encyclical is not the same as divine mercy in Holy Scripture.

In the Encyclical God's mercy is universally given unconditionally "from generation to generation" to all because it is "as a perfection of the infinite God itself infinite." In Sacred Scripture, however, mercy is for all "them that fear him (God)" (Lk. 1:50).

The Encyclical ignores God's sovereign freedom even in mercy. In the biblical history of salvation God's "infinite mercy" is revealed also in His sovereign freedom. That can be seen in the Old Testament especially in the free choice of Israel as the chosen people of God from all the peoples of the world (Ex. 19:4ff.). In the New Testament the followers of Christ and the new chosen people of God (I Pet. 2:9ff.).

St. Paul comments on God's freedom in mercy also in the 9th chapter of his letter to the Romans. God can give and refuse His grace and mercy in absolute freedom how and to whom He will. "He says to Moses, 'I give grace to whom I will and I have mercy on whom I will have mercy'" (Rom. 9:15). or, "God has mercy on whom He will and leaves in his hardness of heart whom He will" (Rom. 9:18).

Certainly Christ is the incarnation of the merciful love of God. But Christ did not leave out of His picture of God the image of the angry judge (Mt. 22:7 & 13). In Romans we read (Rom. 1:18), "God's wrath will be revealed from Heaven over the godlessness and injustice of men who by their injustice oppress God's truth." In Holy Scripture sinful man is shown to be completely dependent on God's Redemption (Rom 3:9ff.), who requires Faith for him to be justified. There is no inner or exterior obligation for God to give an unconditioned mercy. God only gives His mercy to the contrite sinner. That is what the Good news of the Gospel says. We simply cannot remove from our revealed image of God what does not suit the concept of an unconditioned mercy for all.

Similarly, because God's mercy is "infinite" it does not remain unaffected by man's sins like some divine fate so that it can only be restricted or rejected by an *a priori* redeemed and justified man if he does not want it. In Sacred Scripture God is not so trapped by His infinite merciful love that He passively leaves the limitation or rejection of His mercy to man alone and must put up with what man decides. In Jesus' parable the merciful master has the full freedom to withdraw his mercy from the unmerciful servant and gives him up to the torturers full of wrath (Mt. 18:23-34). Also in the Gospel we hear about eternal damnation with which God can punish (Mt. 25:48). God is infinite love and mercy but nonetheless not a beggar who is dependent on the reciprocal mercy of man.

Since the power of divine mercy can only be "limited" by man's stubbornness and lack of willingness to convert, so continues the Encyclical, the Church therefore preaches conversion. Using these premises conversion is defined as follows (*DiM* 13.6):

> Therefore, the Church professes and proclaims conversion. Conversion to God always consists in discovering His mercy, that is, in discovering that love which is patient and kind (cf. I Cor. 13:4) as only the Creator and Father can be; the love to which the "God and Father of our Lord Jesus Christ" (II Cor. 1:3) is faithful to the uttermost consequences in the history of His covenant with man: even to the cross and to the death and resurrection of the Son. Conversion to God is always the fruit of the "rediscovery" of this Father, who is rich in mercy.

Once again this text only superficially *appears* to present the Church's teaching. In reality the Church is said to preach conversion on the basis of the universal giving of grace: For conversion is, as the reference to "the history of His covenant" shows, the discovery of the mercy of the God who is joined and remains indissolubly united to man in eternal faithfulness to His covenant of grace *ab origine*. What conversion means in this context has already been shown in the parable of the Prodigal Son (cf. *DiM* 5.6; 6.1-5).

The Pope continues with his teaching on conversion (*DiM* 13.7):

> Authentic knowledge of the God of mercy, the God of tender love, is a constant and inexhaustible source of conversion, not only as a momentary interior act but also as a permanent attitude, as a state of mind. Those who come to know God in this way, who "see" Him in this way, can live only in a state of being continually converted to Him. They live, therefore, *in statu conversionis*; and it is this state of conversion which marks out the most profound element of the pilgrimage of every man and woman on earth *in statu viatoris*. It is obvious that the Church professes the mercy of God, revealed in the crucified and risen Christ, not only by the word of Her teaching but above all through the deepest pulsation of the life of the whole People of God. By means of this testimony of life, the Church fulfils the mission proper to the People of God, the mission which is a sharing in and, in a sense, a continuation of the messianic mission of Christ Himself.

The state of perpetual conversion is called "the most profound element of the pilgrimage of every (!) man and woman on earth" as if it were obvious. The text then clearly presupposes the universal giving of grace.

But when "authentic knowledge of God" is the source of conversion then the preaching and accepting of the true faith is the absolute condition for conversion. Abstraction is, however, made of conversion to the God of Jesus Christ in an obediential act of faith. "Conversion" is simply generalised. It is simply the state of "every man and woman *in statu viatoris.*"

Thence the Pope comes to the problem of Christian ecumenism. He sees the Church's ecumenical task in the framework of divine mercy of all and conversion as the following text shows (*DiM* 13.8):

> The contemporary Church is profoundly conscious that only on the basis of the mercy of God will she be able to carry out the tasks that derive from the teaching of the Second Vatican Council, and, in the first place, the ecumenical task which aims at uniting all those who confess Christ. As she makes many efforts in this direction, the Church confesses with humility that only that love which is more powerful than the weakness of human divisions can definitively bring about that unity which Christ implored from the Father and which the Spirit never ceases to beseech for us "with sighs too deep for words" (Rom. 8:26).

The Second Vatican Council has thus brought about a fundamental ecumenical change in the purpose of the Church, a conversion as it were: From now on the Church relies on God's mercy and on the humble confession that only love can lead to unity. This new dogmatic statement signifies the ecumenical change in the conciliar Church. *Dives in Misericordia* does not talk about religious ecumenism in any greater detail. That has already been done in *Redemptor Hominis.* The principles are valid "in a similar way" (cf. *RH* 6.1).

Actually it is obvious that the Church's ecumenical task is first of all a question of truth and faith. That is why until the Second Vatican Council the central point of the Catholic Church's ecumenical efforts was the struggle for the unity of faith. The "humble confession" of the conciliar Church is nothing less than the giving up of a position that previously was thought to be impossible to give up.

This was clearly defined before the Second Vatican Council by Pius XI in his Encyclical *Mortalium Animos* (1928). It may be summarised as follows:

Since there is only one true religion which was revealed by God there is only one way for non-Christians to truth and life: the Way of conversion to the religion and Church of Jesus Christ.

Since there is only one Church which was founded by Jesus Christ there is only one way for non-Catholics: conversion and return to the Catholic Church. The full Catholic Faith without any restrictions or omissions is the bond of unity. Love on its own cannot bring separated Christians together.[10]

The difference between the Church's teaching before and after the Council, between the Encyclicals of Pius XI and John Paul II could hardly be greater.[11]

14. The Church seeks to put mercy into practise

At the beginning of his great concept of equality and reciprocity in mercy as the formative principle of a "culture of love" for the whole of humanity, the Pope places the fifth beatitude from the Sermon on the Mount (*DiM* 14.1):

> Jesus Christ taught that man not only receives and experiences the mercy of God, but that he is also called "to practise mercy" towards others: "Blessed are the merciful, for they shall obtain mercy" (Mt. 5:7). The Church sees in these words a call to action, and she tries to practise mercy.

The practise of the beatitude begins in each case with the individual (*DiM* 14.1):

> Man attains to the merciful love of God, His mercy, to the extent that he himself is interiorly transformed in the spirit of that love towards his neighbour.

This "evangelical process" is more than just a one-off con-

[10] For *Mortalium Animos* and the Church's position after Vatican II see Part I, pp. 1-19.

[11] *Ibid.*

version but a way of life, a sign of the Christian calling. Merciful love shows itself as "unifying and also elevating power" "which, by its essence, is a creative love" (*DiM* 14.2)

Reciprocity also belongs to the essence of this creative power (*DiM* 14.2):

"In reciprocal relationships between persons merciful love is never a unilateral act or process." The giver always becomes one who receives.

The Pope quotes Christ as the authority for this principle (*DiM* 14.3):

> In this sense Christ crucified is for us the loftiest model, inspiration and encouragement. When we base ourselves on this disquieting model, we are able with all humility to show mercy to others, knowing that Christ accepts it as if it were shown to Himself (cf. Mt. 25-40). On the basis of this model, we must also continually purify all our actions and all our intentions in which mercy is understood and practised in a unilateral way, as a good done to others. An act of merciful love is only really such when we are deeply convinced at the moment that we perform it that we are at the same time receiving mercy from the people who are accepting it from us. If this bilateral and reciprocal quality is absent, our actions are not yet true acts of mercy, nor has there yet been fully completed in us that conversion to which Christ has shown us the way by His words and example, even to the cross, nor are we yet sharing fully in the magnificent source of merciful love that has been revealed to us by Him.

The principle of reciprocity in mercy whose theological heart is the relationship between Christ and man has already been dealt with in some detail (cf. *DiM* 5-9).

Before the Pope develops his theories for society from this principle he rejects in an unusually vehement way the views of those who do not accept his theory in a threefold crescendo (*DiM* 14.4):

> Thus, the way which Christ showed to us in the Sermon

> on the Mount with the beatitude regarding those who are merciful is much richer than what we sometimes find in ordinary human opinions about mercy. These opinions see mercy as a unilateral act or process, presupposing and maintaining a certain distance between the one practising mercy and the one benefiting from it, between the one who does good and the one who receives it.

This false opinion which does not take reciprocity into account is also presumptuous. For (*DiM* 14.4):

> Hence the attempt to free interpersonal and social relationships from mercy and to base them solely on justice.

This opinion which separates mercy from social relationships and bases them alone on justice is not only presumptuous but also contradicts the whole of revelation. For (*DiM* 14.4):

> However, such opinions about mercy fail to see the fundamental link between mercy and justice spoken of by the whole biblical tradition, and above all by the messianic mission of Jesus Christ.

According to this there is a fundamental link between mercy and justice. This is described in more detail (*DiM* 14.4):

> True mercy is, so to speak, the most profound source of justice. If justice is in itself suitable for "arbitration" between people concerning the reciprocal distribution of objective goods in an equitable manner, love and only love (including that kindly love that we call "mercy") is capable of restoring man to Himself.

This definition of the bond of love between mercy and justice is further strengthened by the addition of the definition of equality. The Pope finally gives the following definition (*DiM* 14.5):

> Mercy that is truly Christian is also, in a certain sense, the most perfect incarnation of "equality" between people, and therefore also the most perfect incarnation of justice as well, insofar as justice aims at the same result in its own sphere. However, the equality brought by justice is limited to the realm of objective and extrinsic goods, while love and mercy bring it about that people meet one another in that value which is man himself, with the dignity that is proper to him.

According to this we may thus define mercy and justice and their mutual relationship in the Encyclical as follows:

– Mercy is the "most profound source of justice" (cf. *DiM* 14.4).

– Christian mercy in the most perfect incarnation of equality between men in the realm of dignity.

– Justice is the most perfect incarnation of equality between men in the realm of extrinsic goods.

According to this the fundamental structure of mercy and justice is equality. The difference is of a merely modal nature.

What is peculiar to the Pope's position is seen when one compares it with traditional theology:

– In classical Catholic moral theology mercy is love of neighbour due to compassion.[12] The one giving help descends to his neighbour suffering want, in order to relieve him of his suffering. Christian mercy is not only natural compassion but love itself which turns to him in need out of the love of God.

---

[12] Hieronymus Noldin, *Summa Theologia Moralis* (Heidelberg 1944, Editio 28), II, p. 90: "*De natura misericordiae.* 1. *Actus caritatis erga proximum in miseria constituto est opus misericordiae seu eleemosyna generatim sumpta.* 2. *Misericordia est virtus moralis, qua homo ex commiseratione inclinatur ad sublevandam alienam miseram. A caritate igitur eo differt, quod haec proximo universim vult et procurat bonum ex benevolentia, misericordia autem ei, qui in miseria est, ex compassione. Miseria enim proximi naturaliter movet ad compassionem et compassio ad sublevandam miseriam.*"

[13] Joseph Mausbach/Gustav Ermecke, *Katholische Moraltheologie* [*Catholic Moral Theology*] (Münster 1959, 11th ed.), II, p. 147.

It is seldom properly understood by non-Christians. Compassion is condemned by some (Stoics, Nietzsche), overdone by others (Schopenhauer influenced by Buddhism).[13] Christian mercy, therefore, implies neither a perfect equality nor a perfect reciprocity. But already Cardinal Wojtyla held the opinion that love can only exist between equals.[14]

– Justice is defined in classical Catholic moral theology as "the lasting direction and inclination of the will to respect the rights of others, to give to the other what is his due." As cardinal virtue it is "the fundamental characteristic of all social thinking with the inner intention to respect one's neighbour as someone with rights and the behaviour which results from this." According to scholastic canonists justice proper falls into three categories:

a) commutative (*iustitia commutativa*); this governs the relationships of individuals (citizens) between one another (*relatio partis ad partem*);

b) distributive (*iustitia distributiva*); this governs what the government does with regard to the citizenry distributing the common goods to individuals (*relatio totius ad partes*);

c) legal (*iustitia legalis* or *generalis*); this governs the duties of the individual towards society, subordinates towards the State and Church (*relatio partis ad totum*). This also includes social justice (*iustitia socialis*) or justice for the common good.[15]

The Pope makes no distinction within justice itself, he makes only a modal separation from mercy. Justice is, according to his definition, simply the most perfect equality between men in the realm of exterior goods. His principle is not "everyone his due" but "to all the same."

The Pope notes that through "equality created by love the differences between men" are by no means removed. Rather

---

[14] Karol Wojtyla, *Liebe und Verantwortung. Eine ethische Studie* [*Love and Responsibility: An Ethical Study*] (Munich 1979). Original in Polish, Lublin 1960; Revised edition, Cracow 1962. Fundamental theses of this work reappear often in *Dives in Misericordia*

[15] Joseph Mausbach/Gustav Ermecke, *op. cit.*, III, p. 11.

by exchanging the rôles of giving and receiving men make each other richer and by this "unite people in a more profound manner" (*DiM* 14.5). This close bond leads to the desired aim: to mutual brotherhood of all men in one Family of Man (*DiM* 14.6):

> Thus, mercy becomes an indispensable element for shaping mutual relationships between people, in a spirit of deepest respect for what is human, and in a spirit of mutual brotherhood.

The principle of equality and reciprocity in mercy is therefore the shaping element in the creation of a social order of universal brotherhood.

Thus the Pope has given the principle of a social order that represents the ideal of a perfectly communistic family of man in universal brotherhood and equality in the realm of man's dignity and property. Perhaps he would also like to imply that the idea of "communism"—although the Encyclical does not mention it—was also godfather to the early Christian communities who as we read in Acts (Acts 2:44ff.), "And all they that believed, were together, and had all things common. Their possessions and goods they sold, and divided them to all, according as every one had need." Though St. Paul still had to take collections in his communities to support his brothers in the faith in Jerusalem.

The Encyclical applies the principle step by step to the concrete reality. It begins with the closest circle of human relations:

Reciprocal, merciful love must be present above all amongst those who are close to one another: amongst friends, spouses, parents and children but also in education and in pastoral care (*DiM* 14.6).

The principle of equality and brotherhood in reciprocal mercy is not just for the small circle but also has a wider application: for a human culture of love (*DiM* 14.7).

The aim of a "culture of love" (Paul VI) in the social, cultural, economical and political arena is only to be achieved if the principle of justice is completed and corrected by the spirit of merciful love (*DiM* 14.7):

> Certainly, the Second Vatican Council also leads us in this direction, when it speaks repeatedly of the need to make the world more human, (cf. *GS* 40) and says that the realisation of this task is precisely the mission of the Church in the modern world. Society can become ever more human only if we introduce into the many-sided setting of interpersonal and social relationships, not merely justice, but also that "merciful love" which constitutes the messianic message of the Gospel.

According to this the Church's mission consists of realising merciful love by the principle of reciprocity and perfect equality in the realms of man's dignity and property in order to "make the world more human."

The Pope adds a new element to all this: reciprocal pardon. Man's world can only become "more human" when we bring to all human relationships "the element of pardon." "A world from which forgiveness was eliminated would be nothing but a world of cold and unfeeling justice" in whose name only the rights of the strong would be respected (*DiM* 14.8).

That is why it is one of the Church's most important tasks "to proclaim and to introduce into life the mystery of mercy, supremely revealed in Jesus Christ" (*DiM* 14.9). But in order for there to be no misunderstanding regarding the universal human character of this mystery, the Pope continues (*DiM* 14.9):

> Not only for the Church herself as the community of believers but also in a certain sense for all humanity, this mystery is the source of a life different from the life which can be built by man, who is exposed to the oppressive forces of the threefold concupiscence active within him (cf. I Jn. 2:16). It is precisely in the name of this mystery that Christ teaches us to forgive always. How often we repeat the words of the prayer

> which He Himself taught us, asking "forgive us our trespasses as we forgive them that trespass against us," (Mt. 6:12)...The consciousness of being trespassers against each other goes hand in hand with the call to fraternal solidarity...If we were to ignore this lesson,what would remain of any "humanist" programme of life and education?

The idea of constant forgiveness is specific to the Gospel. In the Encyclical it is made a general premise: Together with merciful love it is made a "source of life" for "all men" a general principle of "brotherly solidarity."

In order to preclude any misunderstanding about continual forgiveness, it is said later in the Encyclical (*DiM* 14.10): Even when Christ requires us to forgive "everyone every time" (Mt. 18:22) "it is obvious that such a generous requirement of forgiveness does not cancel out the objective requirements of justice" (*DiM* 14.10).

Earlier it was said that mercy is the most profound source of justice, now the requirement to forgive adds a new dimension to this relationship. Now (*DiM* 14.11):

> the fundamental structure of justice always enters into the sphere of mercy. Mercy, however, has the power to confer on justice a new content, which is expressed most simply and fully in forgiveness." However, "fulfilment of the conditions of justice is especially indispensable in order that love may reveal its own nature.

The Encyclical justifies this by quoting from Scripture the parable of the Prodigal Son again (*DiM* 14.11):

> In analysing the parable of the Prodigal Son, we have already called attention to the fact that he who forgives and he who is forgiven encounter one another at an essential point, namely the dignity or essential value of the person, a point which cannot be lost and the affirmation of which, or its rediscovery, is a source of the greatest joy (cf. Lk. 15:32).

Thus the Pope exposes the dogmatic heart of his whole concept of universal giving of grace. Then the dignity of the "value of the person" is the inviolable image of God which each man has. That is why the Encyclical does not just apply this to the Church but to "all men of good will" (cf. introduction to Ch. VII).

In conclusion the Pope calls upon Christ, the whole of Tradition and the last Council to justify his theories (*DiM* 14.13):

> The basis of the Church's mission, in all the spheres spoken of in the numerous pronouncements of the most recent Council and in the centuries-old experience of the apostolate, is none other than "drawing from the wells of the Saviour" (cf. Is. 12:3).

This happens in a spirit of evangelical poverty: "Ye have freely received, give freely" (Mt. 10:8). By this it is even clearer "that God is rich in mercy" (*DiM* 14.13).

Critical Review:

The Pope's thoughts may be summarised thus: The principle of equality and reciprocity in mercy do not only determine the "easy law of the plan of salvation," but also that of the new world order.

The "culture of love" in *Dives in Misericordia* is the Pope's answer to the picture of our present threatened generation. This picture has the spiritual profile of the successful ideas of the liberal enlightenment. Our generation's consciousness is marked with the ideas of the unity of the human race and liberty, equality and fraternity "beyond all artificial borders."

These influential ideas and powers of our generation are taken up by the Pope into the mission of the Church of today filled with the ideas of equality and reciprocity in mercy and with the aim to make the world ever "more human" and thereby to create a culture of love for man.

The theological foundation of this "culture of love" is the

axiom of the universal giving of grace. All the main ideas in our generation's consciousness are made theologically more profound and in this are changed in their very roots and transformed:

If all men are the adoptive sons of God then all humanity is an anonymous Christendom; then there is already latently present the unity of man in grace; then the general brotherhood of man consists in the brotherhood of the adoptive sons of God; then freedom of opinion, conscience and religion is anchored in the untouchable basic value of human dignity; then justice is the most perfect incarnation of equality of all in the realms of dignity and goods; then all can draw "freely" from the "source of life" which the Encyclical has opened for all. There is absolutely no mention of a requirement of faith or baptism in the Church's messianic mission of today. The declared aim is just to "make the world more human" (cf. *DiM* 14.7). All that is left of the substance of Christ's mission is this "*humanum*" adapted to the world. But without the conversion to the Father of Jesus Christ, without faith in Jesus Christ, without the reception of baptism any "*humanum*" remains but a utopia.

CHAPTER VIII

THE CHURCH'S CRY FOR GOD'S MERCY IN OUR AGE*

Chapter VIII is the grand finale in which the Encyclical's *leitmotifs* sound out once more and are taken up into the prayer of the Church. While all around the present generation is threatened in a terrible way the prayer of the Church becomes a "cry for God's mercy."

15. The Church calls on the divine mercy

The Encyclical takes up the themes of Chapter VII and turns to the closing theme (*DiM* 15.1):

> The Church proclaims the truth of God's mercy revealed in the crucified and risen Christ, and she professes it in various ways. Furthermore, she seeks to practise mercy towards people through people, and she sees in this an indispensable condition for solicitude for a better and "more human" world, today and tomorrow. However,...never...can the Church forget the prayer that is a cry for the mercy of God amid the many forms of evil which weigh upon humanity and threaten it. These "loud cries" (cf. Heb. 5:7) should be the mark of the Church of our times, cries uttered to God to implore His mercy, the certain manifestations of which she professes and proclaims...in Jesus crucified and risen.

In a continual repetition the Pope describes the Paschal mystery as the "perfect revelation of mercy" as "love which is stronger than death and sin and every evil" which "lifts man up when he falls into the abyss and frees him from the greatest

---

* Title in the English translation, "The Prayer of the Church in Our Times."

threats" (*DiM* 15.1). But this revelation of mercy has in the mission of the Church still only the aim, "to make the world more human" (cf. *DiM* 14.7). Thus divine mercy in the work of the Redemption is brought down to the level of something purely natural to make a more human world.

Considering the inhumanities committed in the world today the "solicitude for a better and "more human" world, today and tomorrow" (*DiM* 15.1) is great, very great.

But Christ's work of Redemption is much more: It is primarily the infinite glorification of God in time and eternity.[1] For it is the Redemption of the world and justification of the sinner who is in absolute need of Redemption "through God due to faith in Jesus Christ for all who believe in Him" (cf. Rom. 3:22ff.). To communicate *this* mercy of God to man is in the first place the "Church's messianic mission."

Christ's duty to mission for His Church is not, "Go unto the whole world and make it more human. Preach to man his great dignity of being an adoptive son which he hath from always and cannot lose."

Rather the duty to mission which Christ gave His Church until the end of time, including today's Church is, "Go into the world and preach the Gospel to every creature. Who believes and is baptised will be saved who does not believe will be damned" (Mk. 16:15ff.).

The difference between these two missions shows clearly the difference between Christ's Church in the Gospel and the Church in the Encyclical. The Encyclical mentions at no point the necessity of faith, baptism and the Church for salvation. The reason is obvious: If man is saved *ab origine* then all the messianic mission has to do is "to make the world more human."

To complete this understanding of what mission is the last article of the Encyclical adds the prayer: Considering how our generation is threatened the Church must not forget "the prayer

---

[1] Ludwig Ott, *Fundamentals of Catholic Dogma*, p. 185.

that is a cry for the mercy of God" and "these 'loud cries' (cf. Heb. 5:7) should be the mark of the Church of our times" (*DiM* 15.1). It is a cry for mercy not just in the Church's name but "also in the name of all the men and women of our time" (*DiM* 15.2). This prayer of the Church for mercy in the name of the whole of humanity must also be understood in the sense of "this document" (*DiM* 15.3):

> Everything that I have said in the present document on mercy should therefore be continually transformed into an ardent prayer: into a cry that implores mercy according to the needs of man in the modern world. May this cry be full of that truth about mercy which has found such rich expression in Sacred Scripture and in Tradition, as also in the authentic life of faith of countless generations of the People of God.

Once again the reader is told that the teaching of "this document" is nothing but "the full truth" which has been expressed so fully in Sacred Scripture and the Church's Tradition. But this identity simply does not exist:

Already as Archbishop of Cracow Cardinal Wojtyla made clear in his book *Sources of Renewal* (1972) that the Second Vatican Council was a second Pentecost that the Church was enriched in its faith regarding the Church and Christ's mysteries.[2] He repeats the same in *Sign of Contradiction* (1979).[3]

---

[2] Karol Wojtyla, *Sources of Renewal.* A study of how to put the Second Vatican Council into practise (first published in Polish, Cracow 1972), pp. 14ff. On p. 19 we read, "Putting the Second Vatican Council into practise, that is, the conciliar renewal, must begin with the principle of the enrichment of the faith." This "enrichment is simply the more perfect participation in divine truth" (p. 19). The enrichment of faith is thus to be understood in the sense of *fides quae* as well as *fides qua*: "This enrichment which I consider to be the basic requirement for the Second Vatican Council to be put into practise is to be understood in two ways: as an enrichment of the content of the faith which is contained in the Council's teaching and as an enrichment—which proceeds from this content—of the whole existence of the believer who

In *Redemptor Hominis* he announces as Pope the new "full universal consciousness of the Church" (*RH* 11.1) as well as the new "more perfect knowledge of the mystery of Christ," which was made known to Christendom at the opening of the Council (*RH* 11.3).[4] At the beginning of the Encyclical *Dives in Misericordia* he calls "the deepening and manifold enrichment of knowledge of the Church" and the "opening to Christ" a "fruit of the Council" (*DiM* 1.4). This enrichment of the faith means in fact the new teaching of universal salvation just as it is presented in "this document." This new teaching is neither to be found in Holy Scripture nor has it ever been expressed "in the authentic life of faith of countless generations of the People of God."

In "this document" there is by no means a development of the previous faith of the Church but from an alteration based on the principle of the "double revelation" there follows an alteration of Scripture and the Church's Tradition based on the principle of universal salvation.

This new view of universal giving of grace is presented to today's man in an urgent way at the end of the Encyclical. Then it is said that the deeply felt hurtful rejection of love of God by today's man leads to an "attitude of petition." What this petition means is described as follows (*DiM* 15.4):

> At the same time it is love of people, of all men and women without any exception or division: without difference of race, culture, language, or world outlook, without distinction be-

---

belongs to the Church. This enrichment in the objective sense which represents a new stage on the way of the Church to the "fullness of divine truth" is at the same time an enrichment in the subjective, human and existential sense" (p. 22). Concretely this enrichment means a more perfect knowledge of the mystery of Christ and the Church, *i.e.*, all men are saved and justified and the Church of the living God unites all men. Humanity is the invisible Church.

[3] Cf. Part I.

[4] Cf. Part II/1.

> tween friends and enemies. This is love for people—it desires every true good for each individual and for every human community, every family, every nation, every social group, for young people, without exception. This is love, or rather an anxious solicitude to ensure for each individual every true good and to remove and drive away every sort of evil.

This universal, unconditioned and limitless love "for all men without exception or division" beyond all boundaries of race, culture, language and religion marks the Pope's personal behaviour strongly and very visibly. It is one of the most noticeable external signs of his pontificate.

The Pope himself reveals the most profound impulse of his actions when he asks his contemporaries who do not share his faith for understanding for his actions (*DiM* 15.5):

> And, if any of our contemporaries do not share the faith and hope which lead me, as a servant of Christ and steward of the mysteries of God (cf. I Cor. 4:1) to implore God's mercy for humanity in this hour of history, let them at least try to understand the reason for my concern. It is dictated by love for man, for all that is human and which, according to the intuitions of many of our contemporaries, is threatened by an immense danger. The mystery of Christ, which reveals to us the great vocation of man and which led me to emphasise in the Encyclical *Redemptor Hominis* his incomparable dignity, also obliges me to proclaim mercy as God's merciful love, revealed in that same mystery of Christ.

The Pope's care comes therefore from his limitless love "for man" and "for all that is human." This all inclusive love for man has a theological source: It comes from the consciousness of "the incomparable dignity of man" which "Christ has preached to us through his revelation of the Father and His merciful love" (cf. *DiM* 1.2). It is in this mystery of universal salvation which the Pope's universal love of man is founded.

That is how it differs from the love of neighbour in the New Testament: It preaches to man his incomparable dignity as an adoptive son of God, his inviolable dignity as the image and likeness of God. It announces to man the Father's mercy who has given him an inviolable value of being man *ab origine*. But it ignores for this reason man's true nature. It hides his true nature of being in Original Sin, his absolute need of redemption and the necessity of faith and baptism (*necessitas medii*) for salvation. It does not tell man that when one is confronted with Christ, the Crucified and Risen One one must make a choice, that faith in the Redeemer and baptism are required from him, that accepting or rejecting faith and baptism means eternal salvation or damnation (Mk. 16:15ff.). From this theological source came the Church's care for man before the last council and drove her to mission the world.

The last cry of the Church for mercy for our threatened generation contains the prayer (*DiM* 15.6):

> that the Love which is in the Father may once again be revealed at this stage of history, and that, through the work of the Son and Holy Ghost, it may be shown to be present in our modern world and to be more powerful than evil: more powerful than sin and death.

What does this prayer for the Father's love, the presence of the Son and the Holy Ghost to be revealed "once again" mean? This is explained in the final cadence of the Encyclical (*DiM* 15.7):

> In continuing the great task of implementing the Second Vatican Council, in which we can rightly see a new phase of the self-realisation of the Church—in keeping with the epoch in which it has been our destiny to live—the Church herself must be constantly guided by the full consciousness that in this work it is not permissible for her, for any reason, to withdraw into herself. The reason for her existence is, in fact, to reveal God, that Father who allows us to "see" Him in Christ (cf. Jn. 14:9). No matter how strong the resistance of human history may be, no matter how marked the diversity of contemporary civilisation, no matter how great the denial

> of God in the human world, so much the greater must be the Church's closeness to that mystery which, hidden for centuries in God, was then truly shared with man, in time, through Jesus Christ.

Even this last sentence in the Encyclical is in itself ambiguous. But in the sense of "this document" it is quite clear. The "mystery which, hidden for centuries in God, was then truly (*revera*) shared with man, in time, through Jesus Christ" it is the mystery of the universal giving of grace.

Doubtless the changes introduced by the Second Vatican Council represent "a new phase of the self-realisation of the Church." These changes, however, are in no way a continuous development of the old faith of the Church. Rather the self-realisation of the Church since the Council has for its foundation, according to the Pope, a new understanding of revelation which she received from the Holy Ghost at the last Council. She has undergone an unusual "enrichment of the faith": the revelation of the universal giving of grace.

It is the clear teaching of Sacred Scripture and Tradition that the general revelation was closed with Christ and the twelve Apostles (D 2021).